I0492402

"Having POWER makes me more valuable and more indispensable."

Cindy Bahadur-Ramkumar

"The POWER of my innate beauty is more important than your opinion of me."

Cindy Bahadur-Ramkumar

Walking in MY TRUE POWER

Life Happens!!!

Author

Cindy Bahadur - Ramkumar

Copyright © Thursday 2nd July 2020 Cindy Bahadur-Ramkumar

Walking in MY TRUE POWER

All rights reserved.

No part of this publication may be reproduced, stored in a retrieval system or transmitted, in any form by any means, electronic, mechanical, photocopying, recording or otherwise, without prior written consent of the publishers, author and copyright holders.

The author and publisher have made every effort to ensure the information contained in this book was correct at the time of going to press and accept no responsibility for any loss, injury or inconvenience sustained by any person using this book.

All contents of this book are the author's professional opinion; the author recommends you must seek legal advice when managing your business, company organization, your personal and professional life.

ISBN - 10: 1983917184

ISBN - 13: 978-1983917189

DEDICATION

Dedicated to the many who have given their POWER away and opted for the feeling of powerlessness over the feeling of being powerful.

Dedicated to those who decided for the first time in their life to reclaim their POWER and to use the POWER they possess within to become who they were truly meant to be.

Dedicated to my mom Angela Bahadur and dad Ramchand Bahadur, your love and support for me transcends oceans and continents.

Dedicated to my husband Neal, who tirelessly stands by my side,

and to my kids, Oñalín, Milano and Alezandro, your love, respect, admiration and kindness to me, reminds me every day why I choose to live and choose to write.

"The ability to feel POWERFUL is a choice, we can either choose to be subservient and timid
or
we can choose to be fearless and bold."
Choose your POWER wisely.
Cindy Bahadur-Ramkumar

ACKNOWLEDGMENTS

Thank you to those persons who crossed my path in life from 2010 to 2020. Directly, indirectly and without knowing, you have had a part in helping me perfect my art of writing and strengthening my personal aura. I had many personal conversations with friends, acquaintances, co-workers, family members and myself. Through your conversations with me, I allowed myself to laugh, to live and to love again. Each conversation gave me a different perspective on life and allowed me to broaden my horizon, succeed and grow again and again.

I have been blessed to travel the world, meet intelligent, smart persons, laugh and cry uncontrollably. I am fortunate and blessed to have what I have, be who I am and to experience many new experiences.

I respect, and am forever greatful for the blessings life has given to me through the vessels of human interactions.

Thank you again to everyone who assisted me, enlightened me and helped me in this journey of life without knowing and indirectly assisting me to write my 7th book, Walking in MY TRUE POWER.

*"The only garden I attend to is mines.
All my life I have tended to everyone else's garden.
It's time to reclaim my POWER,
and
tend to my garden (life) and my garden (life) only."*
Cindy Bahadur-Ramkuma

FOREWORD ABOUT THE AUTHOR

Over and within the past few years, I realized that there was a burning, insatiable desire inside of me to be more me and a better version of me. As I grappled with the thoughts of who "the TRUE ME" was and is, I realized very quickly that I wanted to be more of whom, I knew deep down inside was a version of me.

I knew I was becoming very tired and exhausted, both mentally and physically. I was giving a part of me to every person I met, but I was not being a whole me to me. Also, by the time I decided I wanted to be "ME" I was too tired to even position myself to be "ME", then life took over and life happened. Life led me down a very dangerous, disappointing and sad path for a ten year period. My biggest challenge was keeping myself afloat daily, with a smile on my face, hiding my world from the world.

I am a mom, to three beautiful teenagers, who demand my time constantly and often says bluntly, "Mom when you have time for me, please let me know, as you never have time".

I am a wife to a loving husband, a silent partner, whom sometimes I forget needs my time equally.

I am a working woman and a business woman. I am also a home-maker.

Finally, I am somebody's daughter.

"Reclamation of your POWER is often feared by the person or the environment within which you are reclaiming your POWER from. Do not be afraid to reclaim you from the world and from yourself."
Cindy Bahadur-Ramkuma

FOREWORD ABOUT THE BOOK

The idea for this book came about because I was exhausted with being everyone's gofer. I am extremely good at what I do, both in my personal and professional life, however life was becoming empty and I could not figure out why it was becoming empty, even though success was attainable and always on the horizon with every new undertaking, life became empty and always felt empty.

I adopted the belief that "life happens", and I began to coin every encounter in my life as "life happens". The rate and frequency with which "life is happening" was becoming uncontrollable to me and I felt like I was letting the reigns and controls of my life go.

Almost every day, I felt life Santa Claus, always giving to others, the more I gave, the more I had to give because it was an unprecedented expectation that I had set with others. I felt like I was Santa leading my reindeers except that the reigns that controlled my reindeers were blowing in the wind and the reindeers were taking me in all different directions. There was no control, no direction and no sense of belonging to anything or anyone anymore. I was losing control and had lost control.

One day, I could not take it anymore, my frustration level was blatantly recognizable at home. I put on my gym clothing, my sneakers, earbuds in my ears and told my husband I will be back in a while and I left. Normally, every evening for an hour, I went for a walk to clear my mind and refocus. It was a task I looked forward to and I delighted in, but on this day in 2018, it was not a walk to clear my mind or to refocus, it was a walk of frustration, a walk of fed up of life, a walk of fed up with people and a walk of what in the world is going on with my life. I was losing control and I did not know how or why.

As I began to walk, my mind took me to a myriad and history of many dark places, my eyes soon overflowed and tears automatically burst through below my sunglasses. Luckily for me, wearing sunglasses was a bonus, I cried as much as I wanted to because my eyes were not visible to others. I kept walking and walking with no clear defined path in mind, my tears kept flowing like a broken bathroom faucet, unable to be repaired and I did not know how to stop the tears. I walked and cried for an hour and forty minutes, with only busy bustling thoughts flowing through my mind. Without a doubt, passersby would have thought I was crazy, they would have taught that a crazy lady was walking and crying without any sound and without stopping.

Finally, after what seemed like an eternity, I stopped by a public bench, located close to a bus stop and asked myself what in the world am I doing with my life? It was at that moment, sitting on that lonely bench at the bus stop on Bovaird Drive in Brampton at 7.30 p.m., I realized that I was giving my power away. I did not even know what I meant by using the word power or how to define the word power, but I knew I was giving away my power to others.

My ah-ha moment came when I realized, the more I gave my power away, the less control I had on my life and the crappier I felt.

I realized quickly that my life was about power, and that the only person who controlled and had control of my power was me. The power that I controlled was something that was innate and within. I initially did not know that I had power or possessed power or even that power was a word used to describe myself and my relations with others. I always thought to myself that life was dealing me an unfair hand as always and I had to play the hand the best way I knew how, with the cards that were dealt to me.

I also realized, in that split moment, that I was giving away my power each and every time to every person I came into contact with because I wanted to please them, to satisfy them and indirectly I wanted their unconfirmed approval of me, however I still had no clue I was soliciting approvals from others about my life.

As soon as this idea popped into my head, I realized immediately I wanted to share it with the world. I wanted to share my story and my life of power. I wanted to make sure that every person in the world understood that we feel the way we feel because we allow others to take and steal our power, directly and indirectly, knowingly and unknowingly, and if we can control this, we can control the manner in which we live and the successes we attain.

I now fully understood that we can control our internal peace, our internal noise and our way of living by managing the power we possess inside of us. Of course a book was my only method of sharing my story, it was the only method I knew how to capture everything succinctly.

Upon arrival to my home, I told my husband about the thoughts of my "new book" and his response was "not another book again, even if I said no, I know you will still write it", and from that day of sadness and frustration the idea for Walking in My TRUE POWER was born.

"There is POWER in Permission. Give yourself Permission to have the POWER to be who you were truly meant to be."
Cindy Bahadur-Ramkumar

TABLE OF CONTENTS

Introduction

When I began writing this book I was not sure about the book's outcome or its content. I knew deep down inside of me there was a process to be defined and I equated the process to the exchange of something for something. I finally figured out that in order to achieve something, in order to acquire something, in order to do something, something had to be given in exchange for an attainable end result.

The more I thought about it, the more I was fascinated with the driving force pushing humans to exchange something for something else. I could not quite put my finger on it, neither could I explain to anyone or even myself what my brain was leading me to materialise. I knew that I was truly fascinated with the ability to have my thoughts transcend and turn into favourable outcomes. Every time I thought about something I found a way to allow it to manifest itself into reality. I very quickly realized I was tapping into something interesting and delicious and I was more driven to find out what I was tapping into.

When I began to write the book *Walking in MY TRUE POWER,* many thoughts were popping into and out of my mind. None of the thoughts were coherent, neither were the thoughts making any sense. I only knew I was exchanging something for something which ultimately became an intended outcome.

As I began to dig deeper, to complete a deep dive into my own thought processes, I realized that I was trading my inner thoughts for an intended outcome. Soon I began to equate my thoughts with the word power. After that, I quickly realized that whenever I gave up something I was giving away an innate part me which was defined as the power that I possessed inside of me, I called it my own personal power.

For example I was exchanging my power with food. When I needed to feel good, I ate. I was trading a feeling for a tangible outcome. I was trading my ability to feel comfortable, and my ability to feel whole again to food. I found comfort in food and powerless when I did not have that comfort feeling. To feel good I would consume more food, which meant I was giving away my control and the control I had over myself to food.

Quickly I realized, everything in life that we own, that we feel, that we can see, comes from the directive of power. In order to feel powerful we trade one for the other. I have noticed in many situations when a person needs to feel powerful, that person dominates and asserts their power to a more subservient person. The more subservient person becomes docile and submissive to the powerful person. Walking in my true power means that inside of me, deeply embedded inside of me is the word and feelings associated with power, finding that path to assert my true power means that I own the right to walk in my true power.

Some days I am very successful in recognizing the power that I possess inside of me and I am able to take control of my life and the power that I possess inside of me. I am able to take charge of conversations, I am able to take charge of decisions that I make in my life, I am able to deal with difficult people, and I am able to walk with a certain greatness and confidence. On days when I feel powerless, I lack confidence, I lack the ability to make decisions, I am very decisive, and there is no clear path defined for me.

Walking in my true power means that I have found something inside of me that guides me to make decisions in the best interest of me in my life. Walking my true power means that I have made a conscious decision to utilize my power with only me in mind. Walking in my true power means I am not willing to trade my greatness for substandard. Finally walking in my true power means that I take control of my life, I take control of my thoughts, I direct my mind to the thoughts that I want to think, I choose the people that I want to have conversations with, I make choices selfishly in my own interests without hurting anyone else, and I assert my confidence by knowing that there is power in everything that I do and I say, and I have to decide to whom I give my power. Walking in my true power means that I am no longer a victim of circumstance, I am no longer a victim of people, I am no longer a victim of my thoughts, I am no longer a victim of my past, and I am the queen of my now.

Finally, as I finished this book I was very hesitant to let it go. I began this book in 2018 and was it completed in May 2019. I did not want to let the book go, neither did I want to publish the book. I would ever so often go back into my manuscript and read and reread, edit, add more content to my manuscript, but I was never ready to let go of it. I did not know why I did not want to let it go and to this day I am not sure why I am afraid to let it go. I know there's a story to tell, I know there are many lives to be healed, I know there are many lives to change, and I definitely know there are many lives to touch through my voice and through my book. Over the last year, because I have discovered what my true power is, I decided that I wanted to share what my true power was with others and help them find and discover their true power. I knew the secret to finding my true power and I felt it only worthwhile to help every person that I meet find their true power. It was not a very easy process for me and I have helped and assisted many, many, many persons both males and females find their true power, even without publishing my book.

I believe the only reason why I am afraid to let the book go is because the book shows my vulnerability, and I am afraid to demonstrate my vulnerability to others. Sometimes the most powerful are also protected and afraid and I too am afraid of sharing myself with the world, however I have made a commitment that through my book **Walking in My TRUE POWER**, I am dedicated to changing many lives by showing them that we all have that power inside of us that will guide us and will show us the path that we are destined to live, we just have to know how to find that power, how to tap into the power, and how to use that power that we possess inside of us for the selfish betterment of ourselves.

Walking in My Power to Please

Many days I find myself walking in the power to please. I am not sure why I need to please anyone and everyone I meet, yet I find myself daily trying to please everyone. During my continuous self-introspection, I realized that my innate ability to please comes from my upbringing, my interactions with others and my sheer necessity to avoid conflict, discord and disarray with others.

Reflecting deeply into my upbringing, a few standout thoughts comes to my mind. My escape from poverty, my need for a better life than the life I currently live and a strong desire to fit into my current environment, all emerge as attention grabbing thoughts. Maybe it's that strong desire to fit in with everyone else which has indirectly forced me to become a pleaser, non-conflictual, agreeable, likable person. This is the power of pleasing.

I saw my mom taking care of my dad and her family. She became a stay at home mom when we were kids. She left the wealthy affluent life, for a life of poverty driven by love. I never understood her why, but it was apparent and evident every time I saw her look at my dad or he looked at her, there was a deep undying love in their eyes.

As I grew older, I began to understand my mom's why, and why my mom loved my dad in his entirety. Hers is a story of fairytale love and romance. My dad drove by my mom's home in San Fernando many, many, years ago. I think it was in 1973. My maternal grandparents being very traditional and long-timeish, believed that a village raised a child and that girls should never embarrass their family, in fact having a girl child was seen as a burden to the family and the only intention of a mom and dad in the era of the 1900s to 1970s, was to ensure that any girl child they had, be married off quickly so as not to bring shame to the family.

"When you come into your TRUE POWER, you never feel bad about the things you do not want to do."

As modernized and affluent as my maternal grandparents were, they held on to their traditional values, especially the traditional East and West Indian Hindu values. From my best recollection of stories told by my mom to me, my dad would pass by my mom's home in San Fernando, and would wave to her whenever he saw her. I also understood my mom would make herself presently visible in the veranda or porch so that she could wave to my dad as he passed by.

My mom told me my maternal grandma used to tell her that out of shame for her girl child having an interest or expressing an interest in the opposite sex, a marriage needs to be arranged. My maternal grand mom called my dad one day when he was passing by and asked my dad "What is your interest in this girl?" As soon as my dad expressed his interests in my mom, my maternal grand mom asks my mom if she liked my dad, to which she replied "Yes". From what I understood, no sooner than they both said yes, a wedding was arranged. This is an example in Trinidad and Tobago of the traditional Hindu custom of arranged marriages.

I believe my maternal grand mom went to my dad's mom family home to discuss the marriage. She was petrified of the way they lived. They lived in real poverty, no beds, no inside washroom, no toilet, an outhouse, their home was made of wooden structure and their flooring was made out of mud. The flooring was "leepayed" daily by my aunts and uncles, in order to keep the flooring level and smooth with a glistened shiny look.

My maternal grand mom could not fathom the extent of poverty that my dad's family lived in. It was an unbelievable level of poverty for a city person to wrap their head around. On my dad's side there was no running water, there was no inside toilet. The house was in a dilapidated condition and there was no electricity.

Minus the material items, my dad's family, a family of ten

kids, had a huge amount of love. I believe for my maternal grandma there was no turning back. The in-laws had met, a wedding date was arranged, both parties agreed to be married and that was it. A wedding was to be had, with all the frills and fancies and a bride was leaving a rich beautiful life to move into a life of poverty, filled with love.

Even though my mom lived in poverty at my paternal grand mom's place, and she said goodbye to the rich life she was brought up into, she never looked back, she always looked forward, she always had a dream and she supported my dad's dream. There was not a day in my life that I saw her angry, sad, or even upset. She had a heart of gold and a mind filled with endless possibilities. My mom's entire life was dedicated to the up-liftment of her husband and her kids. Looking back on my life, my only thoughts are that I follow in her footsteps and that I also walk in the power to please.

There are thousands of occasions in my life, as part of my self-retrospection, I reflect on and about my past and I now fully understand that I built my life pleasing others. I possessed an ability to please each and every person that has crossed my path, be it from entertaining and making food available to them in an instance, to setting up meetings on a whim, to working late hours just to make sure that I satisfy all interested parties. I remember the many days where my ability to please was so heightened that my kids, my husband and my family took a backseat to my work and career, my desire to succeed and my desire to please everyone.

Sometimes, in fact most times, my sole intention was to satisfy, and to make my friends, family and guests happy that I did not realize I was creating moments and events where I was pleasing others and not myself. I, without knowing it, was so driven to make everyone happy, to please everyone, that I would be working ten hours in my work office, and another five to six hours at home during my personal time with my kids and my family present in person, but absent in my mind. When my kids sought my attention, the only response I provided each and every time was "To give me a minute I am working on something I will be there with you shortly".

Now I look back on these situations and scenarios in my life and I realize I very rarely provided a solution to my kids needing me, as I kept working and working in order to fulfil respective parties and work colleagues needs, while my family took a back seat and became second fiddle.

I became a pleaser and was a pleaser all my life without even knowing that I was, and never fully understood why I was being very diligent to please everyone.

Did I acquire this once desirable and admirable trait which has now become an undesirable trait for me from my mom? I learnt the ability to please from a very tender young age, watching and observing my mom try to make everyone happy in her life, forgetting her needs and her wants and watching everyone else's need supersede hers.

Is my mind subverted, and secretly playing games with me? Does my mind make me work diligently to please others in order to obtain workplace acceptance or social acceptance?

Is it that my innate nature is too ensure every person that I come into contact with and every person's path that I cross, I have to ensure that they are happy? I know now, indirectly all I am doing for myself is working to please everyone else except myself.

I am one hundred percent sure and I can one hundred percent guarantee that there is no pleasure or appeasement for myself in pleasing others. I work extremely hard and I work with the gratification of others in mind, to ensure I obtain the desired results.

I am walking in the power to please and I need to make a concerted mindset change to accept the fact that the only person I need to please is myself. Through the power of pleasing myself unconditionally, only then can I please others conditionally. For many, many years of my life, I have worked the opposite way, I please others and worked to please others and not please myself. Now that I am writing this book, I realize that walking in the power to please is all about having the power innately to please myself, to be fulfilled inside, to glow from the inside and let that light shine on the outside.

It took me many years to understand that I had the power to please myself all the time within me, however I never took the time or made the effort to define who I needed to please and why. Once I finally decided that having the power to please was about having the power to please myself and make myself happy, I was better able to position myself to please others, I was better able to be of service to others because I was of service to myself first.

"TRUE POWER means looking at life through different lens."

I began to find gratification with doing things to please myself and make myself happy. I would take long walks, go out by myself, listen to music, immerse myself in loud music, dance and enjoy every moment and most importantly I found a safe space where I hung out with myself, I cried as much as I wanted to, I laughed as loud as I could and shouted my joy to the world without care for anyone else.

I finally figured out that there was immense power in pleasing, and I could control and divert my pleasing power to whoever I wanted, especially to myself. I finally opted to divert my power of pleasing to myself and decided that the only person in the world that I needed please and to make happy was myself, for when I am happy I can transcend my happiness to everyone else who crosses my path. I am committed to making myself happy first and walk in my own power to please, pleasing myself first. I have finally decided to put myself first in my life.

"There is POWER in living life and embracing life the way it should be lived, that is POWERFUL."
Cindy Bahadur-Ramkumar

Walking in the Power of Anger

People get angry for many different reasons, some get angry because things do not go their way, because there is no favourable outcome to what they are searching for, because the other party may not be in agreement with them, and finally because they need to prove a point to others which sometimes while attempting to prove a point is at the detriment of hurting others in the process.

Many ask what is anger and what causes anger? My interpretation of these questions is different from the explanation provided by many. I look at anger as something innate and inward which is built up inside of us and needs a place and a direction to come out to. When it does come out, it comes out to the first person that we make contact with intentionally or unintentionally. Many times during our angry moments we say things that we do not mean and we unintentionally hurt others with our intentional words.

Being angry causes us to burn bridges with others, to hold resentment within, to lose valuable friends, to say hurtful words, and to act in haste, which the majority of the times in hastiness we have no control of and we have lost control of all our mental facets in that split second and short moment.

When I look back at my life there were many times that I lost control and I said things that were hurtful especially to my loved ones. Being angry caused me to take out my anger on my closest love ones even though they were not the cause of my anger. I took out my anger on my loved ones, because indirectly I knew no one else will entertain my anger episodes, or venting episodes, or lack of control episodes except my loved ones. I remember they were many times during my marriage that I would get angry for non-family related matters, on those occasions I unconsciously chose to vent and express my anger to my spouse, and when he was not around I took my anger out on my kids not because I wanted to but because no one else was available to entertain my anger.

Over the last ten years I have learnt to curb my anger and my frustration with life, my disagreement with the world and my frustration with everyone else. I have learnt to curb my anger by using an approach which provides tremendous value to me, and has helped me become a better person not for others but for myself. I created this new approach and it has done wonders for my life and has aided and helped many women to evolve and blossom into all they were truly meant to be.

I am not sure how this approach came to me. It may have come to me in one of my personal internal sessions with myself where I decided that I wanted a better life and a more fulfilled life, which I needed to chart that path for myself. In my search for a more fulfilled life, I made a decision to "rise above". Rise above was personal to me and it meant that I was no longer going to keep myself at the same level of others. It also meant that I am no longer comparing myself and my life to others but I am comparing me to the me that I want to be.

With my technique of "rising above" I have learnt and was able to control my anger. I began to apply this technique every time I would become infuriated with people, with circumstances, with situations, with outcomes, and with unpleasantness that I did not like. I began to train my mind to rise above. This meant that I was no longer playing at the same level of others, it also meant that I was positioning myself to always be one level above everyone else for the sake of my mental happiness, mental peace, calmness and personal internal satisfaction. I was no longer playing anyone's game, and I was no longer dancing to anyone's drums except the beat of my own drums.

"Be in sync with the energy that has POWER."

I wish I had discovered this technique that I created for myself during my earlier years. When I think back of how many years I have robbed myself of my own personal happiness and internal satisfaction it breaks my heart. I know I can never change words spoken out of anger and I can never remove the pain I have caused my loved ones during my fury of anger moments. However, I know how to correct my future mistakes, and as such, I continue to rise above, I continue to delight in my internal happiness and I continue to revel in my own peaceful satisfaction that I am positioned where I need to be in my life.

I taught many women how to rise above and how to build themselves up when they are broken down. I have shown many how to reclaim their old life and create a new life awaiting for them, and I have even shown myself how to reclaim the life that was intended for me rather than to live the life that everyone wants me to live.

Some of my most powerful words are "I do not want to play in your dirty water". I trained myself to look at anger situations and anger moments as a pool of dirty water. I taught myself to have no interest in playing in dirty water. Whenever I got angry with someone I was playing at their level and I was playing in their dirty water. I was playing in their mess and creating a mess for myself. Now, I fully understand and have no interest in becoming angry, and have no interest in playing at anyone's level except mines and most importantly I am no longer interested in playing in anyone's dirty water. I am only interested in playing in my clean water and the water which belongs to me.

When I talk about dirty water I am talking about anger, hatred, animosity, jealousy, vengefulness, and hurtfulness. These are qualities people often possess when they are evil, have ill-intentions and malice towards someone. These are some of the qualities which make people get angry. When I say I am no longer interested in playing in someone's dirty water, I mean I am no longer interested in playing in their pool which contains words which are negative in nature and behavior. I am now more apt to look for clean water and to remain in clean water. When I speak about staying in my clean water I am speaking about remaining calm and collected, I speak about being able to remain in my world, in my space, maintain my inner peace and aura, reveling and delighting in happiness and living life to the fullest.

If I allow someone's dirty water to enter into my clean water or I allow their dirty water to cross over and mix with my clean water, my water becomes tainted and dirty. Once my water becomes dirty, I move further away from my purpose and power in life and I gravitate towards qualities that are negative in nature.

I learnt over a period of time how to manage my anger. I learnt how to not get angry, I learnt how to remain in my world and not let the shenanigans of other people's world affect mines. Throughout it all, I learnt how to build my power, how to reclaim my power and how to maintain my power. I understood every time I swaddled and paddled in someone's dirty water I was entertaining their negativity and I was losing my power to them and I was giving away my power to them.

Once I began to maintain my composure, once I began to rise above and once I remained in my clean water and protected my water from dirty influences, I understood I was reveling in the power that I possessed. I learnt how to enhance my power of anger and how to make my anger and anger moments work for me. I learnt how to rise above in anger and I learnt how to extract power from anger.

I finally learnt to walk in the power of my anger. It was a difficult process, however once I began to master it, I was able to walk in the power of my anger faster and I began to revel in the power of my anger expeditiously.

There is power in anger. We can use that power to destroy others and indirectly destroy our soul and our inner being by feeding and festering negativity to our soul, or we can learn to enhance and support our soul and inner being by allowing our power to guide us, to help us rise above, to help us choose wisely, to help us converse smartly and to teach us to maintain our personal space positively by keeping the aura around and inside of our personal space clean, focused and positive.

There is power in anger, we just need to know how to use the power for the benefit of ourselves in a positive manner.

"There is POWER in living life and embracing life the way it should be lived, that is POWERFUL."
Cindy Bahadur-Ramkumar

Walking in the Power of My Skin Colour

"Oh my God Telma (not her real name) you are just as black as Angela and Ram's children". These words resonated with me throughout my childhood life as I did not understand and I did not have clarity into understanding what was being said, but I knew that we were called "black" by someone else.

Initially I thought Aunty was speaking about us being burnt by the sun, because we were sunbathing in Store Bay, Tobago. We were merely kids, aged no more than five or six years old. Slowly I began to realize it was the colour of our skin that she referenced as black, and not the sunburnt that we experienced, because we relished in and enjoyed the sun, sea and sand. The reality and irony of Aunty calling us black, was not because we were sunbathing and got sunburnt, it was because in her eyes we were considered black kids or kids of African descent, even though we were not of African descent, we were of East Indian descent.

As young children, as kids, our minds were consumed with

thoughts about playing on the sea shore, basking in the glories of the warm sea water and hot sunshine. In our minds we were having a vacation in Tobago, a country that we absolutely adored. We were playing with our best friends. These were the only friends we knew as kids growing up. Telma and Tom (not their real names) were my dad's friend kids. My dad and his friend, Uncle Aron (not his real name) were friends long before we were born, hence automatically my dad's friend Aron became my uncle and his wife Katie (not her real name) became my aunt, and his kids automatically became my cousins. We did not know differently, we never knew that we were not blood related, as kids we considered ourselves blood relatives, no one educated us otherwise. For many, many years, until our adulthood life, we believed that Telma and Tom were our blood cousins. As we got older and older we realized that they were children of our parent's friend.

"Connect to your TRUE POWER."

When Aunty Katie made the comment that Telma and Tom "were becoming just as black as Ram and Angela's kids", I was sitting on the edge of the water, enjoying the moments the waves overtook my body. Every time the wave broke on us, we overturned with the wave, and in our childish fervor, we got up and ran towards the waves as it began to recede into the ocean. I remembered my mommy screaming at the top of her lungs for us to be careful, because the tide was pulling us in as we childishly followed the waves. It was indeed funny and hilarious in hindsight that we as kids were completely oblivious to the world that existed around us, or the world that we existed in.

After all, we were just kids, we had no adult responsibilities, and our only purpose in life was to enjoy our time together with our cousins and to have fun with each other. We never cared about the colour of our skin, neither did we care about the non-blood relationship which existed between our families.

The more I pondered about it, as we got older, the more I realized that Telma and Tom were very light-skinned kids, and I was the opposite. I was not dark skinned in colour but I was definitely not light skin in colour. I believed I looked brown, but to me it did not matter at that time.

Again, all I knew and recollect were us five kids splashing around in the water, building sand castles, digging deep holes in the sand and burying each other in the sand, all the while being burnt by the sunshine. We were all just having fun, and with that fun came the price of being labelled as black kids, kids with a specific disliked colour.

This classification, unbeknownst to me, indirectly catalyst my life into looking at skin colour not as a benefit but as a detriment to success and the more I thought about it, the more I realized that by the sheer nature of my skin colour, throughout my life, I have been disadvantaged in life, disadvantaged by society and possibly disadvantaged even in my own family.

I did not know then what I knew now, which was that I was giving away my power to others based on the colour of my skin and based on the way I felt about life. I was also giving away my power of sense of security and well-being to someone who decided that the colour of my skin was more important than who I was as a person.

I remember when my mom got terribly upset with me for the silliest things she would call me names, and all the names would be "black and something" for example "black fowl, black girl, black child". I do not quite remember all the names she called me, however I remembered the word black prefixed to every name calling.

Rightfully so, when I compared myself to my siblings; my brother and my sister, they both were very light skinned in comparison to me. I was the opposite, my complexion was not light skinned, my complexion was brown. This skin colour disadvantage, by the sheer nature of being born of a different completion haunted me and followed me throughout my life.

I was bypassed for specific jobs, ignored by my relatives, compared to my siblings; my brother and my sister and then by my parents at such a young tender age. I decided quickly that being of a lighter skin colour was more important to me than being of a brown skin color.

What annoyed me though, was the fact that both my brother and my sister took after my mom's complexion, she was light-skinned and I took after my dad and his mom's complexion, they were a darker shade of brown. I was quite upset that God, the God that mom took us every week to the temple to pray to and to make offerings to, and the God that mom taught us to pray every day and every night to, was the same God that made me different from my family.

If my memory serves me right, and it did, many times during my childhood, I disliked myself just because of the colour of my skin, as I tried to piece this puzzle of life together. As I grew older, I realized that throughout the many years of mental conditioning by my family, my friends, my relatives, society and strangers, life had taught me that being of a light skin colour was better than any shade of brown skin, a lighter skin colour presented many more opportunities and more favourable outcomes to all situations.

"Find your peace by identifying your feeling of satisfaction and gratitude."

Even I fell into my own mental trap, whereby I myself began to look at dark skinned as non-attractive, and definitely not beautiful. Even unconsciously I would look at males with lighter skin colour as the colour of choice for any long term relationships. My school friends used to chant as if it was some sort of childhood mantra "black girls and black boys make blue kids". I knew I did not want "blue kids", so I was determined to make my future kids a lighter shade of brown, of fairness, of the clearest complexion. I knew from a young age, that the lighter your complexion, the more favourable society's respect was towards you.

I remember when I was introduced to my now husband, then boyfriend, on July 11th 1992, I was definitely attracted to his handsomeness, I could not help but notice that he was of a complexion that I adored and one that I knew everyone would be proud of me to have as my boyfriend. In my mind, there was not any reason why I should say no to such a handsome guy, who had all the qualities, especially the colour qualities my mom adored so much.

I never really was interested in anyone who was of a darker complexion than me and I could not see a person of a darker complexion being beautiful or handsome for me.

Now as an adult, I am mortified that I was mentally conditioned as a child from a young age to view colours of people rather than to view people.

I realized later in life, my negative experiences of complexion and colour had conditioned my mind to view beautiful as a lighter shade, and non-beautiful as a darker shade.

It annoys me to think that all my childhood, my innate power of my skin colour was decided for me, and that I never really had the childhood where I could have reveled and liked the way I looked, or even appreciated the way I looked, because the way I looked already had its predetermined conditions, feedback and comments associated with it.

As a child I never had the full understanding what was being told to me neither did I know the meaning of colour conditioning. To rewind my memory and indirectly listen to Telma's mom talk about us being black, makes me want to scream at her now for classifying us as black, when we as kids were not black, we were sunburnt. I often wondered how did she expect us kids to play on the beach, with umbrellas?

All my life as a child, and a teenager, I was treated very differently by members of my family and persons I came into contact with, on most cases I felt that there was never equal love for each one of us as kids, and because of this nonsense, of being told I was born differently of a different colour, there was less acceptance and tolerance for me. Being born of a different colour made my life very difficult to fit in and to gain acceptance.

"Do not give your POWER to someone who does not have the ability to take control of you."

As I look back on my life, I realize my past makes it very difficult for me to accept that skin colour never had any negative connotation on my present success.

Now, as I grow older, I realize that the colour of my skin was no longer relevant to me being me, or me being successful. My determination and power to succeed, to prove to the world that "I am worthy" was life changing. I decided to choose my own definition of success and make that definition work for me.

I decided a long time ago, I could not change how I was born and I definitely could not change the colour of my skin. I did however, painfully learn to accept that this is who I am and this is what I was born into and this is how I will be forever. It was a very painful acceptance to digest, and took me many, many years to accept this.

However, once I began to accept and love me for me unconditionally and without condition, the colour of my skin became irrelevant. I was more fixated on being me and succeeding as me rather than being fixated on my skin colour.

Now, I never let the colour of my skin define me as a person and I believe because of this definition I was more determined to succeed in life and I was more determined, more than ever to prove wrong the words of a woman, that I held near and dear to me, my "aunt", the woman whose children I embraced as my own brothers and sisters. I was very determined to prove to this woman that we were not black kids and we were just kids sunburnt by the sun.

In our own society, as I write this book the world is filled with many people of colour, who have become and are victims to the words and advice of others. Just as the colour of my skin paved the way my life ought to be lived and led, so to there are thousands and thousands of kids and adults who are disadvantaged, disproportioned, disliked, discriminated, and even disowned by their own family and friends because of their skin color.

Every time I think of skin colour I get annoyed because I remember my mom calling me the "black jumbie", "the ugly black duckling" and everything possible that can be thought of that has the words black in it. I kept asking and telling myself that I was not black, I was brown, my colour was brown, it was brown. I did not know why everyone was calling me black. I did not understand it.

When you are a child, you are told that you have to respect your elders and you cannot question their knowledge or authority much less their spoken words.

At a very tender age in life, I never had the power to do or say anything that offended an adult. I was a child, spoken to, and I had to obey my seniors and elders. Growing up I never had the power of choice to decipher right from wrong. As I grew older, I was able to use my power to differentiate between right and wrong, I was able to make decisions on my own and most importantly I had the power to love me unconditionally, no matter the colour of my skin.

I also had the power to love others unconditionally based

on their skin colour and I gave myself the power of choice, the power to not see colour, the power to see people not their colour and the power to unlearn mistakes taught to me by my elders.

Now I understand that there is power in choosing to respect and admire each other's skin colour and more importantly there is power in being beautiful in my skin colour. Unfortunately, I gave my power away to many others in my younger years because of my perception and non-acceptance of my skin colour, however I revel in the colour of my skin and give thanks every day to be born as me.

If I can relive my childhood, I would tell the child in me to revel and delight in the colour of your skin, I would tell the child in me that there is no shame in being who you are or where you are born into and I would tell the child in me at a very early age in life that the beauty of your skin colour is just as important or even more important than the way others view you and finally I would tell and remind the child in me that you possess immense power within, and that you should never ever give that power you possess within you to anyone else.

People are often scared of the power that you possess within and are more scared when you begin to exhibit traits of how powerful you can become in your own skin colour.

"True POWER is only found when you are honest with yourself."
Cindy Bahadur-Ramkumar

Walking in the Power of Music

The sounds of music is one of the most soothing, relaxing and motivating sounds in the world. I always knew that music possessed power, I just did not know how much power music possessed, neither did I know how to utilize that power to my advantage.

The power of music can either lift my mood and give me the reassurance I need to live and love again, with a strong desire to continue to fulfill my purpose in life or make me angry, upset and dislike life.

There are days when I am totally deflated, upset with life, feel cheated by everyone and feel like I cannot go on anymore, when the burdens borne to me are endless and never ending. Whenever this occurs now, and I feel deflated, I channel my energies towards good feeling music to heal my damaged soul.

I have made up my mind to believe that I have a vested interest in wanting to make a conscious decision to change my mood and my environment, be it in my personal or professional life.

I decided to take ownership of my life and give my power to the music I listen to. Giving my power to music was very trying to me. Even though I enjoyed music, I could not become enveloped in music, no matter how much I tried, because the burdens and worries of life were consuming me and my brain kept directing me to my current reality of my now; my problems rather than the soothing melodies of the songs.

Finally, I surrendered to the power of music, because mentally I needed the solace in my life and because my life was getting out of control and I did not know how to bring it back into control.

I decided that I wanted to uplift my soul. By uplifting my soul I knew I would be uplifting my demeanour. I felt that inside of me, my soul was becoming exhausted. I kept telling my husband and myself that "My soul is tired, my soul is exhausted and my soul cannot go on anymore".

I kept searching for solace and peace but I did not know how or where to find it.

I finally allowed uplifting motivational and inspirational bhajans to enter my soul. I had to make a conscious, concerted and dedicated effort to open my soul. I had to learn how to forget.

As a young girl, I remembered my mom taking us to religious sessions, prayer congregations, temples and nights Yagnas. Although we did not want to go, we did not have a choice, we went because we were kids and it was part of our upbringing. We never had an opinion when it came to worship and prayers because it was a faith we were born into and it was a faith that we grew to love and enjoy.

I can recall the only thing about the faith of Hinduism I did not enjoy was waking up to go to the temple on Sunday mornings or going to Yagnas and Ramayanas late at night, especially when I was tired and sleepy and did not want to attend because I felt I needed to sleep, however I was too young to stay at home, so it was an irrevelant thought anyway.

I always found that when I entered my place of worship, it did not matter what worries or burdens I carried inside of me, especially mentally. For that two to three hours of worship, I no longer had burdens, the burdens seemed to disappear for that short period of time.

There were many times that I would enter the temple with a heavy heart and on the verge of tears, and as soon as I allowed my mind to be consumed by the word of God, my soul overflowed with inner peace and joy, as if I was dancing to a whole different beat, my eyes would swell up with tears and soon it overflowed with the purest, sincerest, loving, humble love for God. As if somewhere in my soul there was a plea to God to take away my burdens without me verbally asking God.

Once the music began to play and the bhajans enveloped the temple, in some sort of miraculous way I felt as if the music was directed to me only and that every word and song being said and sung by the bhajan group was directed to me solely, even though an entire congregation existed. Many times, tears would flow freely from my eyes, and I felt no shame in wiping my tears. This spiritual place allowed me to bear my soul before God.

"Introduce yourself to your POWER and get hooked on it."

Now I needed help and I needed solace and I had to find a method to my solace, a method to the madness I experienced. For the past ten years my life has been in constant turmoil, with occasional fleeting moments of happiness, due to no fault of mines or me contributing to the turmoil. The turmoil was dealt to me and I felt I had to play the cards dealt to me all the while keeping my head afloat of the water, so as not to sink or drown. What I do know and would tell anyone who reaches out to me is that the world is made up of people who are filled entirely with evil intentions. The world is not and will never be at its purest because there are many who live in this world, who seek and find satisfaction by the destruction of others out of pure jealousy for your success.

My solace was found in music, it was the only thing I could have done to keep and maintain my mental sanity. Many days I was on the brink of disaster. There was this one day, when I could not take it anymore, I sat on the edge of my bed in tears. I was really tired with the roller coaster of life and the uncertainties of life. I could hear in the background my three kids playing in their bedrooms and being kids with each other.

Whenever I needed to cry, I would close my bedroom door and cry, literally crying my eyes out, hugging myself while I cried. Once I finished crying, I would emerge and share the joy of my kid's world without letting them see my world.

On this dreadful day in 2012, I decided to kneel by the side of my bed, and poured my heart out to God. During the pouring of my heart out to God, something came to me, it touched me and diverted my attention to my phone. To this day I am not sure what it was.

In that moment, I stopped praying and walked to my phone and decided to play some bhajans. I looked specifically for Lord Shiva Bhajans. I had no idea why and to this day I do not know why. But at that specific moment I felt that the weight of the world and the burdens illicitly bestowed upon my soul were being lifted and removed and I no longer had to worry or have fear. It was such an airy unexplainable feeling, that I kept that thought to myself all these years until now, when finally I am sharing it in my book.

From that dreadful day in 2012, I never looked back. When my soul feels overwhelmed and my body feels burdened by life, I immediately turn my attention to music. Without a question, I position myself and my mind for success.

Be it success in my personal life or success in my professional life, my life is filled with music. I dance to my own beat, I sing as loud as I can and I am completely absorbed by music. Music eliminates negative energy from entering my soul and it stops the burdens of the world from weighing me down. I now make sure that there is music in every part of my home. I purchased many portable Bluetooth speakers and wherever I go, my music goes with me.

Some days I play bhajans, some days I play Chutney music, Indian music, Calypso music, West Indian music and pop music. I choose what I listen to according to the way I feel at that moment.

If my soul is troubled and confused, immediately I gravitate towards bhajans, if my soul needs to dance I play West Indian music, which I absolutely love.

I have found when I allow any this type of inspirational music to enter my body and communicate with my soul, I find my soul very peaceful and the confusion and chaos which had taken over my soul no longer exist for a period of time after the music has played.

My conscious decision to give my power over to music which heals and soothes my soul has allowed me to walk further into my power.

I have even taken my soul fulfilment with music a bit further and have allowed these devotional inspirational bhajans to take over my spiritual being. In doing so, my soul and inner being feels extremely fulfilled and I am better able to position myself mentally for success.

I have always heard about the power of music, but walking in the power of music I love is even more powerful. I get to choose which music I allow into my being and I get to choose which type of music enables the power that already exists within myself. For my readers, do not be afraid to walk in the power of your music and always ensure that you feed the needs of your soul with music that you love and delight in.

"When you feel less vulnerable, it is when you know your TRUE value."
Cindy Bahadur-Ramkumar

Walking in the Power of Time and Moment

Re-collecting from the tender age, possibly of five or as far back as my mind would take me, my mom used to tell me that "Time waits for no one". While I truly did not understand what she meant by "time waits for no one", as I grew older and possibly wiser, I realized this statement to be true and began to understand it. What could have been done, should have been done, and would have been done, we never truly will ever know because the could of, should of and would of, is all past, infinite and unattainable.

To think of time as disappearing, is such an interesting concept, for right now, this current moment becomes the past in a blink of an eye, and every second and every minute lived could never be regained and is considered the past. I always view *Time as a Resource*. Time is the only resource in this world that cannot be bought or sold and it is the only resource in this world that depreciates and is never regained.

I began to train myself to live in this moment, I live for the current moment, and I live to enjoy the moment. I cannot live for the future because the future is unknown and uncontrolled. I cannot live for the past because the past never comes back, the past cannot be changed, it cannot be amended and that sometimes leaves a sour and bitter taste for the future.

When I truly examine time, the only thing I can think about is the present moment. There have been times in my life where I wished time stood still. There are times in my life when I wished I could go back and replay the memories so that I can change the images I see in my mind.

My mom used to say that "Your life is like a tape recorder, every day it is being taped, you do not have the ability to play back the tape neither do you have the ability to fast forward to tape. The only ability that you have, is to press the play button and let the tape recorder play for you".

She always had a way with her words, sometimes we understood her and her analogies and other times her wisdom and analogies just went straight over our heads.

One thing I truly understand from her analogies is the fact that nothing last forever, and if you live in the moment you can make a choice of how you want the moment to end.

In my life there have been moments where I wished I could play back my tape recorder and erase all the bad people that have crossed my path or entered my life. In that moment when evil crossed my path I became a survivor and a victim. While surviving I never knew the ending to my story, neither did I know the ending to my future. But I knew my current moment and I knew how to make the best of what I was blessed with, my current now, my current time.

What I did not know was how to control my moment in time. It took me quite a long while, through trial and error, aggravation and tears, humiliation and sadness, death and loss, sadness and happiness to finally figure out that the only point of my life that I controlled was my current moment, not my past and not my future. I became very determined to make sure no one could steal my moment. I made sure that this was my moment and I was going to protect my moment for as long as I live, because I did not have control over my future outcome but I did have control over me losing my current time.

I never realized how powerful time was until I was physically a victim of time, then I began to control whatever little bit of sanity of time possessed.

I quickly realized that the world was made up of two types of people; those that intentionally set out to hurt you, steal from you and destroy you and those that honestly and genuinely care for you from the bottom of their hearts and with every part of their being.

"Put yourself in a position where you can feel your own POWER."

I choose to surround myself with people who honestly cared for me from the bottom of their hearts. I realized that, in that current moment it was the only thing that I had and I could not let the moment slip away for me, I had to embrace the moment, I had to cuddle the moment, I cried in my moment and I celebrated my moment. I prayed each day that God will give me strength and a bit of extra time to move on and relish my current moments.

No one explained the power of time to me, it took me a while to understand that people can and will try to steal everything away from me, but they could never steal the time that was my now. I realized that there was strength in time and there was power in time. In the moment, the present moment this was the most powerful part of time that I could capitalize on.

My present moment dictated my current, my naivety dictated my past and my love of life would ultimately dictate my future. No one could ever steal my time, my time is extremely powerful and it belongs to me. I will never ever allow anyone to step into my moment and attempt to steal my future away from me because of their selfish desires.

Each and every one of us has had moments in time in our lives where we stop and wonder "what if". We have had moments in which time was very powerful and we were in control of our current situation. There were also moments in our lives where life became uncontrollable and time was slipping by and we had no control over our future.

If you truly understand the terminology "in the moment" and what it means to be in the moment, in the present moment, you will relish every second of your present moment and no one will ever be able to steal your joy or your happiness.

We have to make a conscious decision to stop others from stealing our time. When someone physically abuses you or sexually abuses you or verbally abuses you, that person is stealing snippets of your now time which belongs to only you and no one else.

Consciously you have to take control of your time and ensure the abuser does not steal from you that which belongs to you;

1. your body

2. your spirit

3. your soul and

4. your time

For, in that moment when that the abuser puts their hand on you, that abuser has just robbed you of your present and made your present moment the most horrible past moment. The abuser has just, because of his/her present actions, stolen your future time because you have become enveloped and obsessed with the abuse inflicted upon you.

I have lived through both abuse and evil. I am a true testament to living in the moment and not letting anyone steal my moment and sanity away from me.

In my moment, I give praise and thanks for what I am blessed with, asking for the strength, the courage and the ability to move forward each and every day with confidence because I know, if I do not live in my present moment, I will allow myself to live in my past and I will destroy my future.

Right now, today, tomorrow and every day after, are my moments of my time. While others may try to steal my moments and my present time, they cannot and will never ever steal my now.

I value my power in time, and I am walking in my power of time. I am walking in my power of my moment, and in this moment while many may try, they will never be successful to steal from me, my current time, my current moment, my now.

"There is POWER to live life and embrace life the way you want to."
Cindy Bahadur-Ramkumar

Walking in the Power of Procrastination

Procrastination and procrastinating is not something new to me. It has been something that is sadly engrained within me. I strongly believe that the only reason I procrastinate about doing a task is because the task does not appeal to me, it appears monotonous, it is tedious, I am not into it and I have no interest in completing the task.

I definitely walk in my power to procrastinate because many times I believe that I am an awesome procrastinator. This occurs especially when I do not want to do something that I have no interest in, but I know that it needs to get done. Most times, I more than often do one out of two things; I wait until the very last, last minute to get it done or mentally I condition my mind to believe that it is not important and I just let it slip by the wayside.

Obviously I am a living example of walking in my own power to procrastinate and I believe firmly that only I have the ability to change my power of procrastination and my power to procrastinate by mentally conditioning my mind to get the task done.

My reality is sometimes a dreadful existence. I believe that if I do not get the task done it is not going away. Somehow I have learnt that taking the task away in my mind, or ignoring the task all together never has any good resolutions. Because, at the end of the day or when the task is due, it still has to be completed. My only concern then, is how best to or how soon can I get that task completed. I know it becomes an issue when the race becomes a now, not how best to get the task completed but how fast can I get the task completed.

"Be masterful and mindful of your life experiences."

Walking in my power to procrastinate is a powerful statement. It signals to me that in everything that I do, I possess the power to do it, in such a manner that it is beneficial to me or if not beneficial, it becomes my own detriment and demise.

I remember clearly there were days when on the very last day I would actually spend hours and hours and hours on a task, only to scold myself by saying, had I applied myself to it diligently over a period of time it would have been completed in a heartbeat, however I procrastinated until the end when it was due and I wore myself out both physically and mentally.

The only power that I possess is my ability to not procrastinate, and my conscious ability to deal with my procrastination first hand and get the assigned task done in a timely and efficient manner.

I remind myself daily that I possess the power to do it. I have found a solution to my power, and the solution to my procrastination. I have decided to make a conscious decision to timetable, timeline and document every task that I have to complete. Once I am able to visualize that task, I am better able to apply my acquired power techniques to finalize the end date on that task.

Walking in my power to procrastinate means that I am walking in my power to make a conscious decision to procrastinate or not procrastinate. I have chosen to stay in my power to procrastinate that I no longer want to procrastinate.

I have consciously made a decision that I possess the power to change my method of procrastination and to adopt a positive more upbeat manner to my procrastinating habits. I now timetable in and assign completion dates and follow-up dates on every task I undertake, and hold myself accountable to the completion of my own tasks.

There is no better power that I possess than holding the power to change my life and having the ability to make conscious decisions to change the outcome of the way I want my life to proceed.

I can only reference one example of procrastination even

though there are many more examples that I have experienced in my life. I remember clearly my mom asking me to come home to visit her. My true home and birth home is in a different country. It is a country in the Caribbean called Trinidad and Tobago.

While I had every intention to stop what I was doing and go home to visit my mom, there was that tiny voice in my head which said to me "Tomorrow, tomorrow you will go, tomorrow you will see her, tomorrow you will be able to meet up, tomorrow you can get the task that she wants, it will be done tomorrow".

I made a conscious decision that I will respond to her request tomorrow. Tomorrow was the method my mind adopted to responding to my mom's verbal and personal request. In that instance, I did not realize I was procrastinating, however today when I look back on my life, I was procrastinating.

I procrastinated between what I needed to do, which is my obligation and my duty to visit my mom and my ability to believe in a tomorrow. I made a conscious decision to not be available for her because I let everything else in my life, my then current now, take precedence over my decision to leave my current country (Canada) to visit my home country (Trinidad).

"Your POWER is your happy."

Everything that was going on in my life took precedence over the request from my mom. I did not realize then, but I do now, that I made the conscious decision to respond negatively to my mom's request, when my mom said to me "Can you come home, can you come and visit me, can you come home to see me, I want to see you one last time" by responding "Tomorrow", my response to her was "Some other time", my response to her was "I was busy, I was working, I have other commitments, I have other plans" and I never once put her needs, her plans and her dreams in front of mines.

During my conscious decision to procrastinate and put off what I needed to get done, I lost my ability to say goodbye to my mom, and up to this day, ten years ago that conscious decision that I made in the interest of myself and no one else, haunts me and it is a decision that I have to live with, an unfortunate decision for the rest of my life. I never got to say goodbye to my mom. I never got to respond to her request to come home to see her. Ten years to date, I am fully aware of the decision I made to procrastinate and to not get what I needed to get done immediately, to not complete what needed to get done and to close the door on an open request.

Had I understood the power that procrastinating possessed ten years ago, I would not have done what I did and I would not have denied the request of my mom to see me one more time.

Procrastination rears its ugly side all the time and it is one of those things that destroys lives and livelihoods. It took me a while to understand the power that procrastination possessed and now that I understand that power, I no longer walk in the power of procrastination, I no longer am a slave to procrastination and I no longer allow my life to be held back or kept back by procrastination.

*"There is POWER in Clarity which leads to insight,
euphoria and interest."*
Cindy Bahadur-Ramkumar

Walking in the Power of His Shadow

Walking in the power of his shadow or as an appendage to him is an interesting concept. It can be one of the most powerful shadows to walk in, which can enhance my life or it can be one of the worst shadows to be in which has the ability to destroy my life.

For me I have had the pleasure of being on both sides of the continuum, being in the face of the shadow and being in the shadow. All I wanted to do when I was in his shadow was to get out ahead of it and disappear from it.

"I heal others through my scars, I am enough."

As the old adage goes "behind every successful man is a

good woman". I wholeheartedly believed this adage, because my husband is a true success and represents the epitome of success and hard work. Both my husband and I rose to success together as it should be. Behind his keen and sharp skillset, was someone who managed his business for him. All he had to do was show up, be present and use his skill and charm to succeed. Everything else was done for him, even the miniscule task of ordering mundane business items was done by me.

It was a true pleasure to walk in the shadow. Whatever belief or standard he stood for, I also stood for it. The empire and following he built, we built together. We are a power couple to be reckoned with. We are one of those couples that are very powerful and competitive. I took pride in his work. He is known as Mr. DropTec and I am known as Mrs. DropTec. Together we are inseparable. After all, we built our lives from the ground up, we built our foundation and our family from the ground up and we were both proud of our accomplishments.

There was a lot for me to live up to by walking in his shadow. Wherever I went, I was known as Mrs. DropTec. I was known to people I did not even know. It always felt like wherever I went people already knew who I was, even before I told them who I was. While walking in his shadow was a huge honour, it was becoming a deterrent and detriment to whom I was becoming. I felt like I was an appendage to someone and not a whole to me.

I believe the reality of walking in his shadow, while it was a success also became one of those misfortunes, both at the same time. What my husband and I have been through, physically, emotionally and mentally for the past ten years, to this day, still leaves a bitter taste in both our minds and hearts. Now I am always afraid to walk in his shadow. I am very afraid of people knowing who I am. I have made myself completely invisible to everyone. It seemed as if I had disappeared from my worldly existence and I had cut off communication with everyone; my friends, my family, my co-workers, my work colleagues etc. I did all this to protect my family, to protect my husband and to protect my kids.

When I walk in his shadow, the world knows who I am. Not being in his shadow meant I was free to be who I was supposed to be. The power of his shadow and the power his shadow possesses over me has now dwindled and dissipated. Even though his shadow is still prominent, successful and recognizable to this day, there is a certain amount of incognito I desperately need and seek when I walk in his shadow.

I need incognito when I am around his friends and our business acquaintances. I feel that people are subconsciously relating matters to me, and to an event or a person and I do not want to be associated to. My heart and soul desires to just be known as me.

It is very tough to be known as me, when for twenty-three years of my life I have walked in the shadow of his fame and success. It is tough now to build my own shadow. It is tough now to have a shadow to call my own and even more it is tough now to "exist".

While I learnt to build my own shadow, I also learnt to understand the power of my own shadow. I am at the same time continuing to protect a shadow that once existed.

Walking in the power of his shadow, while there were many positives of walking in my husband's shadow, there was one negative, I never got the chance to build my own shadow. When his shadow dwindled and faded a bit, I had no shadow to fall back on. I clearly remember the day his shadow dwindled, and his light became dim. I sat alone asking myself, how do I move on, where do I go, what do I do? I was always accustomed to working together for business and family success that working alone was intimidating. I had no identity and I had to learn to build one. I did not have a place to call my own and I did not know how to build and create my own shadow. I did not know how to become me and I did not know how to let go of the appendage which held us together.

Slowly I learnt that while there is an obvious benefit to walk in my husband's shadow, there is tremendous benefit in building, maintaining and walking in my own shadow. I learnt that there is power in developing myself to be the best that I can be and to be complimentary to my husband rather than to be an appendage to and in his shadow all the time.

I learnt that I had my own identity and there is power in owning who I am and in being whom I was meant to be also. I learnt that even though there were obvious benefits to walk in my husband's shadow, I also needed to find my individuality and I also needed to find myself and my power.

"Having POWER means getting out ahead of it."
Cindy Bahadur-Ramkumar

Walking in the Power of My Humility

It takes a special type of woman to have the power to be humble against all odds, against all titles, against all materialism and against every negative practice that is meted out to her.

Being wholly humble is a characteristic that few people possess. Many are enveloped in the materialism of the world and define their life's existence by material acquisition. To be humble means to serve at the feet of God. To be humble means to serve each other. To be humble means living a life filled with plenty, but not letting or showing the world that your life is blessed with plenty. Humility means being at the same level of others, and not letting them know that you are not at their level. Humility means treating others with respect, with honour, with sincerity, with dignity and with integrity.

It is a trait that I have always held close to my heart and take pride in. It is indeed a trait that I believe very few possess.

Many have been angry with me because, I, on almost every occasion, I do not divulge who I truly am or my accomplishments in life. I keep silent about who I am and the importance of the impact that I have had in other people's lives.

I remember on my trip to Trinidad in 2017, my mother-in-law was very angry and furious with me. There she was talking and bragging about me and all my accomplishments to everyone she met, which ideally meant she was proud of me and wanted to speak about me while I, on the other hand did not feel the need to talk about myself. She was boasting about me to everyone else (about being an Author, about being a Lecturer, about living abroad, about being a Reporter, about being important) and there I was downplaying all her words to everyone.

She became angry with me in a joking but angry way, telling me that I should be proud of what I have accomplished and that I should tell everyone I meet about myself, and not be shy to talk about myself.

I was not shy, I just felt like I did not want to up-play my accomplishments in front of others who had none or were not afforded the opportunity to do so. To me, it always felt wrong to talk about my accomplishments when my audience had very little or none, or it felt wrong to talk about my books when many never wrote one. It did not matter what I said, or how much I tried to justify my case to her, I was being silly and I should be proud of who I am and where I came from. It was a losing battle with her and I just kept smiling and saying, yes I will let people know about me.

Maybe I am naïve and maybe I just do not get it, but I believe that I am as humble as the most giving soul. I think my underlying foundation, premise and belief, stems from the fact that in a world of many people and opportunities there are still many people out there who need some type of help, guidance or assistance which is not of a financial nature. On my humility mission and sheer nature of humility, I am able to reach out to those who need help without making them feel unimportant, less important, or of lesser value than they are and I strive to ensure each person I meet feels completely valued.

"Make peace with where you are and watch your POWER unfold."

So where does my humility come from? I can only think of the upbringing that my parents instilled onto me and the impact of their kindness to others regardless of the colour of their skin, their size and type of house, or the money in their bank account. My parents are givers and they never hesitate to give to any person that is asking or anyone who extends their hands out for assistance. In fact they always gave regardless of what others had. My parents never judged others, they gave selflessly of themselves, be it money, time or physical strength. My parents are always present, always providing assistance and always giving.

On a family beach trip to Maracas beach, in Trinidad, with my visiting aunty Christina from England, my mom, my grandma were passengers, and my dad was the driver. My aunty Chris requested my dad to stop on the side of the road to purchase some mangoes from a vendor child selling on the roadside.

Not to my surprise at all, my aunty Chris purchased all the mangoes from the child. I asked her, "Aunty Chris why did you do that, why did you buy all his mangoes, we do not need all these mangoes to eat?" Aunty Chris replied "My dear Cindy, if no one purchased the mangoes from the child his mom will not have any money to purchase food". I asked her "How do you know that?" She explained to me that when a parent sends a child out to sell fruits by the roadside the parents are in desperate need of money to take care of their kids. If the parents attempts to sell the fruits for themselves, then the parents will get very little sale, if the parents decides to use their child to sell the fruits, then buyers will feel empathetic for the child and purchase the fruits from the child. That is the power of human empathy. Having money allows the parents to purchase food for the kids.

It took me quite a while to understand this analogy but when I did, I realized that my aunt gave without judging. My aunt Chris was always an angel and my mom considered her an angel.

Aunty Chris also explained to me another story, she said "My dear Cindy if we do not buy the fruits from this child, his mom will get annoyed with him, and when his mom gets annoyed with him she may get angry and she might hurt him out of frustration and then beat him. So, to avoid the beatings let us give this child a day free of anger and punishment", and so she bought all the fruits from him.

One more example aunty Chris provided was the example off a child who was able to sell all his fruits really, really quickly so that he could go outside and play because after all is that not what kids are supposed to do.

I know one of the most important teachings I was brought up with, was the power of humility. I learnt really quickly as I was growing up, that there is no cost associated with giving yourself unconditionally to others and to give what you have to others so that joy is reflected in their faces. Their joy always transcends to internal satisfaction. We are all seeking internal satisfaction. As humans we seek internal satisfaction and acceptance from others.

"Be the change you receive."

I saw the power of humility every day from my mom and my dad. I think throughout life, I acquired the skills and powers of humility from both my parents and from life's taught examples. Earlier on in life I realized that even though material accumulation was important in life, it should never be the most important priority in life. I taught myself to believe material acquisition should never overtake my personality and overtake who I am or who I was supposed to be.

I grew up thinking if we all could make a difference, if I can make a difference in one person's life every day, I have done my job and my duty in this world. If I can help one person in this world, if I can educate one child in this world, if I can teach one adult in this world, and if I can put a smile on one person's face in this world, I have done my job and duty and I have done what I was put on this earth to do.

When I look at myself or think about myself, I believe that I have acquired much and created many. What do I mean by I have acquired much; I mean, throughout my life I have been very fortunate to have a wealth of material acquisitions, I have been very fortunate by the grace of God's assistance to keep a roof over my head and food on the table for my family.

What do I mean by I have acquired many; for me, many is the symbolism of title and prestige I have acquired throughout my life. Throughout my life I have indeed acquired many, many offices, many titles, many company perks, lots of stuff which the ordinary person may not have acquired throughout their lifetime. I believe because I am a very humble person with an old soul, many doors open and continue to open for me for example I have been very fortunate to work for a multitude of multinational companies in my career and lifetime.

Being fortunate to be blessed with such amazing opportunities has shown me the path to humility, for the more I have received, the more humbled and sometimes the more withdrawn I am from society.

One thing though, and the world can testify to this, all the materialism I have acquired throughout my lifetime, all the prestige positions I have held, all the stages I have stood on and all the great people I have met, all this greatness I have been blessed with has not changed me at all, in any form or fashion.

If any, at all, it has made me a stronger woman than I am right now and allowed me to see the world through the eyes of the lesser fortunate and through the eyes of those who have lesser opportunity.

I learnt at an early stage in my life that there is power in humility. I did not realize at that time that words like "power" and "humility" existed, however I learnt that treating others with respect, compassion and care was more valuable that the acquisition of material items.

"Do not turn your POWER over to someone else's ugly behaviour."

In 2010, I was on a flight to Trinidad and Tobago minding my own business, seated by the window in an airplane. My heart was ripped into pieces because I was travelling home to my mom's funeral. I found solace in being seated by the window, and allowing my mind to get lost in a world of memories of my mom.

The window seat is the only seat I ever sat at during all my work or pleasure trips. As much as I was an extrovert, I always felt that I was an introvert, because I feverishly disliked striking up conversations with strangers or others, it was never my strong hold.

I was seated by the window, deep in thought, minding my own business when this older lady, well old lady, she looked about seventy years or thereabouts, sat next to me.

I politely looked at her and smiled, all the while my earbuds were in my ears and my laptop opened in front of me. I always have my laptop with me when I travel. When my mind is overwhelmed, I write to take the thoughts out of my mind and put it into print. Somehow travelling brings out the best in my brain as I am extremely focused and can write the world of words during my flight.

"Hard work just means focus more."

As she sat next to me, she settled herself in and could not resist the urge to begin talking to me, even though I had my earbuds on, she kept talking. Finally, I had no choice but to take my earbuds off my ears and listen to her. Once she got my attention, the only thing I remembered from her six hour conversation with me was her first line to me "You that Reporter girl eh, I read you all the time, I know it was you the moment I saw you and I am happy to sit next to you".

She then took out a newspaper which she just coincidentally happened to have, as if it was her faith to meet me, and showed me my face. The embarrassment and look on my face was so obvious, if I could have disappeared into the seat I would have, because I do not like seeing myself in other people's possession. I had no expression for seeing myself in print. She pointed to a picture of me with pride in her eyes. She was beyond words, and the look on her eyes and in her eyes led me to her soul. Her body was frail and weak, but her soul through the glimmer of her eyes was young and vivacious. She took out a pen and asked me to sign her newspaper at the end of our flight, which I graciously did.

Her conversation with me or rather her conversation to herself with me being the silent converser, lasted six hours. The entire duration of my flight. I knew everything about her, her grand kids, her life, where she was going, who she met, even what she liked and disliked. During that six hours of flight I did not know her name, because she omitted to tell me her name, she was very busy conversing, about everything that she never had time to tell me her name.

This lady was extremely proud that she had met me, she took it upon herself to advise me about everything in her life and she advised me that she will never forget the memory of meeting me.

I, on the other hand came off the flight thinking, God my ears hurt, but I dear not tell her that. What I did was smiled and thanked her for sharing her beautiful life with me. I was a bit relieved inside because she took away all the thoughts of the pain I experienced inside, especially the thought of not seeing my mom one last time.

This old lady was so elated that she met me, I swear she was flying high as a kite. At that time, I did not know about the power of humility, I just knew about humility and to be humble and kind to others. Now I understand that the power I possessed and currently possess to be humble and have humility has touched many lives throughout my lifetime and that, in humility, possibilities are plentiful and boundless.

"Be comfortable with being different and unique."

The power that I possessed to be humble with that old lady, gave her life new meaning, for her that day seemed like it was the most important day in her life. That power of humility that I possess has brought many towards me and has changed the lives of many. My mom's sister always tell me I should be a counsellor, that my words make her feel alive and happy again, that my words give her comfort and that she feels joy when she speaks to me.

My husband on the other hand, tells me that my soul is very old and that all my friends are old people or older people and that he definitely was partnered with an old soul.

Many can testify that after speaking to me, they would not have believed that I am that "important, smart, well known and well established" person, however to me I am just me and I do not see myself in any other facet.

To my husband, I am his wife, to my kids I am mom and to my friends and family I am Cindy. I do not ever walk with titles, awards and affiliations I have acquired throughout my lifetime when I speak to others. I am humble, I am me and I acquired these qualities from my parents.

There is power in humility, once found, many doors will open without asking and many lives will be changed without intentionally doing it.

"TRUE POWER means being satisfied with where you are and being ready and always eager for more."
Cindy Bahadur-Ramkumar

Walking in the Power of Working with a Bully

It takes a lot of tact and diplomacy to deal with a bully in the workplace, a bully at school or in any type of environment. Only the strong minded and strong at heart can survive a bully.

Bullies are intimidating, bullies are non-forgivers and most importantly bullies lack self-esteem and are afraid to trust. This is the reason bullies overpower and dominate conversations in the interest of remaining dominant, controlling and possessive in meetings, in relationships, and even in a crowd.

I have had several encounters with bullies in both my personal and professional life. Throughout my encounters, I have learnt the art of managing a bully firmly, I manage a bully fairly well so much so the nature of the bully does not get under my skin or bother me anymore.

When I was younger, during my high school years, for about five years, 1986 to 1991, I was subjected to bullying on a constant and daily basis. I grew up poor, and did not have as much material items as the other kids in my class, neither did I wear fashionable or flashy items, because my parents could not afford such items. Their priority was focused on obtaining an education and nothing else. My parents always told me "To exit from poverty you have to acquire an education, not just an education but be the best you can be with your education".

This bully girl who was in my class for all five years of high school would constantly harass me about the way that I looked or the manner in which I walked and even my mode of transportation to and from school. This bully was a young girl just like myself, who dominated all class conversations and was always the class clown and the centre of attention, she would seek attention for herself by constantly making fun of me and the other girls in the class.

There were days when she made me cry in class and when I was alone, there were many times she laughed at me and there were times she would humiliate me in front of others. My only need was to survive and remain strong. My method of survival was burying myself into my schoolwork which allowed me to isolate myself from my friends because I could not fit in with them materially.

"There is POWER in thought."

This bully made fun of my level of poverty, constantly laughed at my lack of materialistic items. While in school I never had a backpack, I had a "green book bag", in fact most kids had green book bags because they did not know about backpacks or backpacks were very expensive. This girl laughed at my green book bag every day, she made fun about me and my green book bag. She ensured that the class laughed at me with my green book bag. It was all I knew and all I had though, so I was not sure what else I should do or be doing, because it was the only book bag I had to hold my books.

Besides my green book bag, the most humiliating was my school shoes. Being in an all-girls secondary school, meant that I wore a uniform which included a brown skirt, white shirt and white shoes. My parents could never afford those fancy sneakers for high school, so they purchased a pair of regular white shoes for me. My mom purchased a pair of white shoes called "Jim-boots". It was a Trinidadian pair of shoes from a store call Bata.

At that time Bata shoes was looked down on, and everyone laughed at you when you wore a Bata shoes. My white Jim-boots had worn out and I did not have another pair of shoes immediately for school so my mom gave me her slip-on white flat shoes. It was a normal pair of slip-on white flat shoes, nothing spectacular, except her foot was a size seven and I was probably at age twelve or thirteen a size five. The shoes were bigger than my feet, my feet looked like puss-in-boots in it. I can clearly remember stuffing newspapers at the front of the shoes so the shoes would not fall off my feet when I was walking.

Besides being ridiculed for my shoes daily, the cherry on top of the ice-cream was the ridicule for a hole at the bottom of my shoes, which was worn out from walking. I placed a piece of cardboard inside my shoes, so my white socks would not get dirty while walking. The bully girl noticed the hole in my shoes one day when she was walking behind me and my life became a nightmare after that. I was ridiculed and bullied almost every day after that also.

Because of the level of poverty I lived in, material items and consumer items were not always frequent.

I rose above her bullying, I cried in silence but never in public, I remained withdrawn and kept to myself, I had only one true friend who had my back and made me smile and I kept pushing my way forward academically.

At that time, I did not know about possessing power and manifesting, however upon reflection I can honestly say I maintained my power and control by not allowing her to intimidate me and distract me from my life and my dreams.

"You can only reach your full POWER when your POWER stops buffering, send that signal out and connect to your true self."

Oddly though, in 2005 I received a social media friend request one day. I do not remember the details of the friend request or the social media platform, but I crossed paths with the bully in my adult life and it was thoroughly enjoying to let that young lady know that she bullied me while I was growing up and her only response was she was sorry.

Her sorry did not erase any past memories, it did not make any past pain go away but it did help me understand the minds of bullies. When I got into her mind I realized it was all about power and control, it was all about a person's ability to control that which they were not able to control in their personal life, so they take it out on others to compensate for their lack off or lack thereof in their personal life.

I have been bullied in the workplace countless times and it sickens me to my stomach to know that in the year 2020, bullying in the workplace still exist and worst off, it is propagated in the workplace from middle and senior management, even up to executive management. I have worked in a male dominated work environment and I have noticed males have a tendency to bully females constantly.

In 2017 and 2018, I worked with a tireless bully. This General Manager took pleasure in making women cry at one of the facilities I managed and he especially took pleasure in calling immigrants illiterate and dummies. He is a white guy and I am not sure if his racist qualities meant he was on a mission to bully immigrants constantly or he was just a total bully.

There were days when I would love to really give him my true and honest interpretation of who he is and how much he harassed and bullied others in the workplace and there were days when I decided to rise above the workplace nonsense and think about my family and my bills and let his bullying attitude be. However my conscience got the best of me and my heart bled for the hourly workers. I engaged the Vice President of Human Resources each and every time the workplace bully began his tyrannical rant.

I have always worked in workplaces, where I use my power to work with Human Resources to attend to complaints where males predominately harass, bully, and intimidate women. In fact, I have always been the only female in a male dominated environment.

Bullying and harassment takes place at the senior executive level also from the vice-president to senior management to middle and lower management. The workplace is plagued with workplace bullies.

"Finally I figured out my relationship with me."

Bullying and harassment is highly unacceptable at all levels in the workplace, sadly it existed for me in 2017, 2018, 2019 and I do not expect it to disappear in 2020 and beyond. What annoys me the most, is the fact that men believe they can intimidate, harass and bully women constantly in the workplace.

At the workplace, I felt as if I was subjected to days of colonialism, where the majority of the workers in the workplace were minorities and their executive and middle-management are of specific nationalities.

While minorities (immigrants) in Canada continue to dominate the workplace, minorities are also dominated upon in the workplace, they are verbally abused and harassed. In many workplaces, I have watched men insult women especially immigrants. Most shop floor or manufacturing facilities host many intelligent professional immigrant women who perform work as hourly workers, because they are immigrants and are not able to find employment in their chosen field of expertise, therefore they work as hourly manufacturing workers. I watched men in authority and senior positions, humiliate and call these women retarded, stupid, ignorant, non-educated and worthless employees. The list of abusive words is endless. The voices of these women are often muted.

It breaks my heart every time I witness bullying in the workplace. Given my position of power and authority in the workplace, I am constantly standing up for these women in management meetings and constantly expressing empathy towards these women, making sure that we never call people different names, were all humans.

Bullying exist in the workplace and if anyone out there does not believe it exist, it most definitely does. I want to say to you, open your eyes, realize and accept that it exist because you are pretending and wanting to believe in your mind that it does not exist.

Many times I have heard men shout at women in the workplace and I believe it is unacceptable and it should never be an accepted practice in the workplace anymore.

When I walk in my power, I walk with the ability to have self-confidence, diplomacy, tact, and a certain bit of je ne sais quoi or eloquence that goes with my personal being. I ensure that I am not intimidated by men and I remind myself every day that *I am a POWERFUL Woman.*

Walking in my power of bullying means that I will never allow myself to be subjected to any type of verbal or mental abuse or even harassment from a man in the workplace, it also means that I will no longer subject myself to bullying from anyone, regardless, of age, size, type, nationality, colour etc.

I remember once, the workplace bully began to shout at me in the presence of other co-workers. In my mind, all I could think about was, him over-compensating for his shortcomings by shouting. He insisted that I come into his office so he could carry on the shouting conversation.

My response was "I will not come into your office until I feel I want to come into your office". Honestly, I did not feel that I wanted to subject myself to his verbal abuse or subject my mind to his mental abuse, neither did I feel I wanted to subject myself to his type of foul language and inappropriate behaviour.

He was not at all happy with my response, and he raised his voice even louder, I on the other hand walked away and went into my office and I never looked back. I remind myself daily that I am not going to allow any man to raise his voice to me, neither am I going to allow any man to intimidate me in the workplace.

I stood my ground, held my confidence, held my head up high and I did not allow him to intimidate me. I went into his office on my terms, on my time, and I did not care about how he felt, what he believed or what he thought. It did not matter to me.

I am not afraid of anyone in the workplace and I do not believe that any woman should be intimidated by any male in the workplace, not in the year 2020. We are no longer subjected to the colonial days. We are no longer living in the era of slavery, we are living in a free and democratic society. When I stand as a woman, an extremely powerful woman, I am representing many women without voices. I am standing in my own confidence, in my own power. No one can intimidate me when I am powerful.

"I am satisfied where I am, I am eager for more."

Confidence comes from inside of me, it comes from my ability to manage my words and my thoughts. It comes from my ability to speak eloquently. It comes from my ability to hold my ground. It comes from my ability to command attention and it comes from my ability to be as tactful as possible when in conversation with others.

Build your power one step at a time, one footstep at a time, one thought at a time. I always remind myself, I am one person, I command the respect I deserve, I never let anyone intimidate me. I build my life the way I want it to unfold and I make sure the players in my life are always value added.

I never let anyone bully me anymore. I have been bullied previously in my life. I have been made to feel unworthy. I have been made to feel less than I am and I truly understand how it feels to walk in my power of bullying.

For I do not see a bully, but I do see a person overcompensating for their lack thereof, hence the reason they bully and attempt to intimidate others.

"There is POWER in being comfortable with being different and unique."
Cindy Bahadur-Ramkumar

Walking in the Power of Situational Change

If you can't change the situation, change you. Change your approach to the situation, look for other, more simplistic ways of doing the same task. Change yourself to be out of the situation. Find a solution to your situation. Make you the change.

Life often carries us with it. We get so caught up with life that we tend to forget who we are and what our intended purpose in life is supposed to be. After a while, when we are way in too deep into any situation, we realise that we need help, we are drowning and we need a lifeline. Everything about life is situational. Everything that we do in life is based on situations, on circumstances and on specific moments which occurs to us or of which we are always a part off.

I have positioned myself positively and properly to understand that situations come and go, situations will always arise, every moment and every instance becomes a situation. The method and manner of reaction to the situation defines the outcome of the situation I am faced with or of the situation I am involved in.

I have created and adopted my daily change motto, and when I am faced with any situation; good or bad, I remind myself of my credo:

If you can't change the situation, <u>change you</u>. <u>Change your approach</u> to the situation, look for other, more simplistic ways of doing the same task. <u>Change yourself</u> to be out of the situation. Find a solution to your situation. <u>Make you the change</u>

Your situation would not change unless you change you. Your situation is normally defined as the current environment within which you operate, function or reside. Your current environment could be your home, your workplace, your place of worship, your school etc.

It is the current place which makes you sad, depressed, uneasy, uncomfortable, and you no longer experience the joy of going into it or being in that place. Your current situation was once a livable place, however that environment is no longer conducive to your happiness. Acknowledge that the current situation is no longer good for you and be willing to change yourself out of your current situation.

There is a wealth of power in defining your current situation and understanding your current needs.

Your approach to the situation, defines the intended outcome expected to be received. If you adopt a powerful approach, an approach that has enough hunger and desire for positive change, positive change will take place. If you have a desire for short term change, short term change will take place. You need to have that strong desire for change and a strong desire for suitable change. Your approach and your desire for change goes hand in hand and both approaches work in conjunction with each other.

Approach each and every situation with confidence, with power and with a desire to have a positive impact. Power of situational change is gigantic when use correctly.

When approaching different and varied situations, approach it with calm, composure and structure. Have a plan. It is always a good thing to approach the simple, less complicated tasks first. When you do that, you allow yourself to be free of the burden that is weighing you down and you feel somewhat accomplished because you are completing tasks efficiently and effectively.

Approach bigger more complicated complex tasks with a different plan. Plan a start date and an end date. Plan an in-between accomplish date. Plan various milestones to achieve. When these are completed, the burden of the complicated task, becomes less burdensome and you are able to complete complicated tasks in a timely manner, without even believing the tasks were complicated.

Adopt a plan and a systematic approach to tasks and make the change to the positive situation that you are dreaming off. There is power in every change and there is power in making a systematic plan and following it through to the end.

Sometimes change does not always go as planned, sometimes the situation or the environment is not conducive to change, sometimes the change we desire leaves more to be desired or was not what was anticipated.

When these complex situations arise, it is worth it to make the change out of the situation. There is an immense amount of power in being able to pick yourself up and make a decision that is worthy of changing yourself out of the current situation. This power to make that change comes from within and that is a power that only you possess.

"Use your POWER to bring love, faith and happiness to the lives of others."

There are times when it is not feasible to change yourself out of the situation, even though every instinct in your being is advising you to do it. When such a case arises, the best option is to change yourself to adapt to the situation.

This may mean that you become reserved, that you hibernate, that you have less opinions, and that you become focused on your now and then future. When these situations arise, channel your energies on your future, while enjoying the blessings of the now.

Adopt a grateful attitude in the face of adversity. Find one thing to be grateful for everyday. This will help you focus on your future, take your mind off your current and change your energies to the positive aspects of your life.

When I worked with a bully, I hated that environment every day. I never wanted to go to work. I hated the way he treated women. I hated the way he treated immigrants and I began to dislike everything about that work environment.

Power thoughts were initially born from working there. I had to remind myself daily that I had more power than him and that I was not going to give my power away to him. I was not going to allow him to steal my now. Most importantly, I reminded myself daily that my employees needed me, that there were many paths to cross and there were many hearts and souls to touch. I found my power in my future. I found my power in my now and in my conversations with every pleasant soul I met.

I knew I had to make the change one day. I decided I would make the change when it was right for me, not when the bully decided it was right. The bully was terminated after a year of meeting and working with him. My kind words and ability to maintain my power contributed to his dismissal, because others realized there were different ways to manage a business and organization, of which bullying was not one of those ways.

The powers that be realized that, in order to get buy in and cooperation from all employees, professionalism and kindness were needed, not bullying.

There is power in change, there is power in mannerisms and there is power in behaviours. Choose the power you want to display and make the change according to the power you hold.

"Be the change that you receive."
Cindy Bahadur-Ramkumar

Walking in the Power of My Excuse

This morning I woke up asking myself what is my excuse? What is my excuse for not achieving everything that I believed I could achieve? What is my excuse for not being the best that I can be? How many times can I blame everyone else when a particular situation or outcome does not go my way? Who do I blame when I am exhausted, tired mentally and cannot achieve my goals? These questions bothered me for quite a while, since I really did not have any answers and did not have a clue how to move forward from my stagnant mind.

"Having POWER means getting out ahead of it."

I kept asking myself why can't I not achieve my goals?

How many times do I go about blaming everyone else for me not achieving my goals, the goals that I set out for myself this morning, the goals that I set for myself each and every day? Often I would become really frustrated with myself. I would look myself in the mirror and ask myself what is my excuse today, who am I going to blame today? For at the end of the day when I lay my head down to sleep, I lay my head down in frustration knowing that I have not achieved what I set out to achieve and I could not achieve what I was supposed to achieve.

When my alarm clock went off one very cold morning, at 5.45 a.m., I did not want to wake up. The silent reality of staying in my dream world was far better than living in this world (my existing reality). I would have preferred to close my eyes, snuggle into the warmth of my bed and bury myself into my dreams. At least when I did this, I subconsciously knew that in my dreams and with my dreams I had control, I could awake when I wanted to, I could stop the dreams from playing in my mind if I wanted to and I had a choice to continue my dream or change my dream if I wanted to.

My current reality soon became an everyday reality whereby I could not stop my life from continuing, from playing like a video recorder, whether I liked it or not, my life was continuing each and every second, each and every minute, each and every day, and sadly there were no playbacks or rewinding of my life. I could not change the past second or the past minute. I quickly and painfully realized every second that was in my present, soon became my past, and every minute of my past was irreversible.

I keep asking myself, what is my excuse, what is my excuse for delaying my progress? Finally, I figured it out, after many, many times of trial and error. I figured out my own problem. It was a problem that I was encountering and did not know how to deal with it. After serious consideration of thought, I realized that I was giving away my power to my excuses.

The music of my excuses played every day in my ears whether or not I liked it. It kept playing and I continued to dance to the tune of my excuses and my reality. I got to understand quite quickly, my reality is always my present, my past will never be returned, and my future is undetermined.

Most importantly to me now, is my now reality. I have made a conscious decision to not dwell on and to not refer to my past. When negative thoughts of my past pops into my mind, I take my mind to a happy place which then stops negative thoughts of the past from replaying in my mind. Daily, I remind myself of all the good times and good things I have experienced in my life.

I had the most honest and rude awakening when I realized that I was giving away my power to my excuses daily and not honing in on the power that I held within. I realized that I had the ability to change the outcome of my now.

It was hard to wrap my head around the thought about giving away my power to my excuses, but it was real. Once I understood that everything I did had a certain amount of power within it, I was better able to decide what I wanted to do and when I wanted to do it. Then I was able to eliminate my excuses.

I decided that I wanted control of my power and I did not want to give my power to my excuses. Being very process oriented in thought, and by sheer nature, I put on my process hat and decided that I will find a resolution to my excuses via the process approach.

I looked at my excuses as a separate entity, as a unit. I looked at my power as a unit also. I realized that I had one unit of power and one outside factor. The power was unique to me only. I was transferring my unit of power to my unit of excuse. The more I transferred pieces of my unit of power to my unit of excuse, I was losing my power to my excuses.

My reality was that I was making excuses for everything in my life. I was not procrastinating, I just had a million excuses not to perform, with each excuse better than the last excuse.

"Be more satisfied with life."

Once I realized that I was transferring my unit of power to

my excuses, I was losing my power or losing more of my power to every excuse. I made a decision to now reclaim my power from my excuses. This meant that I was not giving away my power anymore to my excuses, but more importantly I was attacking each excuse and eliminating excuses as I went along. After a short while, I no longer had excuses, because I was eliminating my excuses and making conscious decisions to not give my power away to my excuses anymore.

It took me quite a while to understand that concept of power being transferred to excuses and excuses holding me back from being where I ought to be or performing at the level I ought to perform.

Finally, I mastered the power of my excuses and now I can walk in the power of my excuses. I no longer let having an excuse hold me back. As soon as the excuse pops into my mind and transcend into words via my mouth, I nip it in the bud, give myself a personal talk "Cindy you will not lose your power by allowing your excuses to take over, maintain your power, grow your power and get rid of these excuses".

It has worked so far. It seems like every time my mind hears the word power, my mind is more attuned to strive for more power to make me even more powerful than I currently am.

There is power in excuses, choose wisely the excuse you want to give your power to. Most excuses need no power.

"When you feel less vulnerable, it is when you know your true value."
Cindy Bahadur-Ramkumar

Walking in the Power of Self

It fascinates me to think that it is not that I do not know the power of myself because I teach others about the power of themselves but sadly I forget to spend some time teaching myself about the power of my self.

I realized that the only helpful being in my world is me and myself only. I can choose whether I want to give my power away to someone else and become a victim to them or I can hold on to my power and become victorious. By being a victim to others, I have made a conscious choice to minimize my power within. I could also use the power for my self and make that conscious choice to keep all my power within me and for me, so that I do not become a victim of others in their surroundings.

Being a victim to others, and relishing in my own environment helped me realized the power of self. Self-power is extremely powerful. It is the power of my words and the power of how much I allow others to dictate my value, or to dictate my worth.

For example, my financial worth is dictated by the amount of money I am being paid to complete a task, in simpler terms, it could be the income that I receive for a service that I provide. Financial worth is defined as the exchange of labour and service for money.

When I divide the total dollars I earn into the cumulative hours it takes to get the task completed, I can realize my hourly worth. My hourly worth is the price that I put on myself. The price that I assign to myself for others to pay me, if I decided that my value is more than this price, then I have to increase my price because now I have changed my hourly worth of myself to a completely different value.

"Stay in gratitude, keep yourself grounded in your gratitude."

My self-worth is also mental. It is the opinions others have of me, embedded in their mind, transcended into my mind as a reminder of my worth. For example, when someone says to me "good day you are amazing", that tells me that I am completely worthy of their praise.

When I receive high praise, it alleviates and elevates my mental self-worth. There are days when others perceive or may perceive my self-worth as having little or no value, not because the work is not completed properly, but because the work was completed below the expectation that they had in their mind. In this case my self-worth becomes diminished and lessened in value. When this happens, I mentally I put myself into a hole, I bury myself and I cannot get out of it.

Walking in the power of my self means I have the power to believe and control the way I feel, the way I think, the way I act, the way I behave, the way I perceive others, and the way I believe others perceive me, the manner in which I complete tasks and the manner in which I hold myself accountable for completing tasks, the manner in which I procrastinate to get things completed (because I do not want to complete it and I do not feel the need to complete it and I do not care to complete it) and the manner in which I assign blame to others for situations which are beyond my control.

My unpleasant rude awakening and understanding of my-self power led me to understand really quickly that I control the power of my self and no one else controls my power besides me. I get to decide how I want to feel. This is my power and it allows me to decide how I want to feel. I will not let a bully or a jealous person dictate how I feel or how I should feel in my life. At this present moment I am going to take my power and make myself extremely powerful such that neither a bully nor someone who is envious of my life can take away the power of peace and power of self that I feel inside.

The power of my self tells me that mentally I have positioned myself to conquer the world. I have mentally made up my mind that I will no longer be a victim to my circumstances and situations and I will no longer be a victim to others and expect others to treat me like a victim because of my mindset.

I realized that I have the power in my self and within my self to be whom I am truly meant to be. I have the power to change my current situation, I have the power to make right every wrong and I have the power to allow my mind to control me.

My self-power comes from inside of me, it comes from my internal drive, it comes from my personal determination and it comes from my ability to view myself in a positive light. It comes to my mind reminding me to dismiss all the naysayers in my life. It comes from my ability to walk with my head held high and to dismiss all the negative influences that are penetrating into my life.

My self-worth and my self-determination does not come from someone who dictates or attempts to dictate what I believe, where I should go, what I should be, what I should do and where I should live.

My self-power comes from me deciding to make a conscious decision to answer two questions, about myself; what is the power of my self-worth and what powers does my mind possess?

The ability to control my mind and remind myself that I am able to decide my now, my future and my current is what greatness is all about. Walking in the power of my self means no one can take the power of my self away from me.

The power of self, determines who I am right now in the present moment. The power of self cannot change my past as much as I would like it to. Even though I would like to erase certain situations and certain moments of people from my past, I cannot change my past, I can only walk forward in my present.

I do not know what my future holds. I only have control of my present. My present moment, my here and now, my right now.

My power of my self is more powerful that the environment that I work within. My power of my self will not allow my environment to dictate who I am, dictate what I do or dictate how I become. I made a conscious decision that I and only I will decide how I want my now to be.

The power of my self reminds me that there is no one out there who is more powerful than I am. There is no other person more powerful than I am. There is no other person more powerful than I am about myself right now.

"Believe in your POWER and watch it multiply."

I possess the power to be me and no one, absolutely no one,

possesses that power to change how I am. I am my present and I get to decide each and every day, each and every minute, each and every second, I get to decide how I want my power to be, and no longer will I allow anyone to steal the power of my self.

I have made a concerted effort to make sure that I no longer will allow anyone to decide for me how I live my now. No longer will I allow anyone to tell me how to feel. This is my power and I am walking in my power from today, tomorrow and every day moving forward. It is my power and I make the decisions on how I want to walk in my power of self.

"Do not be afraid to be selfish about your life, selfish about what you want and about what you desire and require, if you are not selfish, no one will be selfish for you, it is your life, OWN it."
Cindy Bahadur-Ramkumar

Walking in My Power of Permission

It seems like everything in life, at some point in time becomes overwhelming and burdensome. Sometimes there are days when I cannot go on anymore. There are days where I feel that I am physically and mentally exhausted and that I do not know how to move forward in life.

On most days it seems like I am taking care of everyone else except myself. I feel like I am fulfilling the needs of every person in my life except myself. I can personally acknowledge that I spend more time on ensuring that I fulfill the needs of every person that I meet, be in the workplace, at home or in my personal life rather than looking after my needs.

I feel as if sometimes my world is spinning and there is no calm in the storm. I know in my heart, that I am doing the best that I can do in every task. I know the end result is what every person wants and they are clearly satisfied with the results and the expectation that they had.

Unfortunately, as I sit back and think about my life and I

take stock of how fast it is passing by, I am realizing that during my very hectic life, I have not given myself permission to breathe, to relax, to smell the fresh air, to enjoy being outside, to spend time with my kids, even just a few minutes to be myself or to take care of myself.

I remember there were many days in my work life when I was thoroughly engrossed in working for companies or for myself where I would always have my lunch about 3.00 p.m., only when I was totally and completely famished. Somehow it always felt like work took precedence over my well-being, even my hunger. It was not a bad thing for my work as I was always delivering, always promoted, always doing an excellent job, however my personal life was suffering and taking a backseat to my work ethic of over accomplishments in my work life.

I remember days when I entered the work place, I was constantly busy and bombarded with work and I was trying to do my utmost best to ensure that all my work was completed and that every person was getting the desired result that they wanted.

In the end, what I do know now, is that those days are not coming back and those times that I did work and completed all the work myself, was only for the benefit of the company that I worked for. There was no explicit tangible benefit for myself except a paycheck and the personal satisfaction of achievement.

Stemming from all of this, I learnt an extremely valuable lesson, all the companies I worked for and left behind, continue to thrive and exist without me, after I left for a new endeavor. I was just the human element (body) on the chair in an office which belonged to me, and all my work and achievements became past because a new person would come in and take over and put their personal flare on all my work and efforts.

I did lose lots. I lost many years of being completely dedicated to the work that I was doing and spending absolutely no time or minimal time with myself or my family.

I realized today, I needed to give permission to myself. One absolutely crazy day, the pinnacle of change arose in my work life. To my amazement, bewilderment, and lack of foresight, I was dedicated and obsessed with my work that I forgot to look after my son's entry application into high school. I was totally engrossed in my work because I love my work and I love what I do and I am passionate about what I do.

"Create your own POWERFUL environment and watch it consume you with POWER."

My desire to be passionate about everything I do, costs me my son's entry appointment into high school. I was blatantly obsessive about work and forgetful about my personal life, that I completely missed the deadline for my son's admission into high school.

It is only when I came home from work, my son reminded me that his high school application needed to be dropped off by me, in person. He reminded me he was obviously too young to drive or take it himself. I stood in amazement and disbelief, as if I was completely lost and numb and in my head, all I could repeat constantly was "Oh shoot! Oh shoot!" I kept asking myself "How could I have been this stupid to miss the application deadline, what am I going to do now, what school will my son attend in September 2019, my God please help me I am so foolish".

I guess my passion for perfection and passion to please everyone else got the best of me and I completely forgot the priorities in my personal life. Because of my lack of giving myself permission to look after me, my son was without a school spot for the new academic year in September 2019.

I had replayed this deliberate act of forgetfulness constantly in my mind over and over and kept asking myself how was I going to let my fellow co-workers cover for me when I was super-busy at work conducting an audit.

In my mind there was no right or wrong answer. On one hand I have already disappointed my son and on the other hand I had to request assistance to cover for me to attend to something that was personal and dear to me during my busiest time at work.

Those who know me, would testify that I never mix my personal life with my professional life and it was quite embarrassing to request immediate coverage because of a personal matter.

Nonetheless I humbled myself, sent an email out to the respective parties and notified my senior in the USA, that I was leaving at 2.00 p.m. because I had missed my son's high school enrolment due to my work commitments or my undying commitment to the work that I am involved in.

There I was now at 2.00 p.m. using a paid toll highway and driving fast but cautious in order to get to the high school that closes at 2:30 p.m. and my drive realistically is an hour and a half away on the regular route.

My mind kept saying, if only God could be merciless and bring forth miracles today, I needed one badly. There was no way that I could get to the school at 2:30 pm. when I am physically fifty kilometers away.

I was determined to drop off my son's application package on time. I arrived at the school at 3.00 pm. I walked into the office and in my mind I knew that this was futile but I had to do it for myself, for my son and I had to make sure that at least I tried.

When I approached the office counter there was this absolutely unkempt lady who looked as if she did not care to see anyone. Politely and humbly I showed her the application package as I was about to explain to her why I was late. She was already all over me, she gave me an earful about deadlines and how she cannot help me and she kept going on and on and on as if to rub salt into a bleeding wound.

I kept apologizing, it was the least I could have done, while saying a million prayers in my head. She did not really care and she was not interested in my sorry story. I am not even sure if she was interested in working there based on her mannerisms. I stood at the counter and I asked her "What am I supposed to do now, when should I come back, and who do I need to talk to?"

She was not able to answer my questions and the more she stuttered the more I asked questions. I was not about to give up, not right now, not after I drove like a crazy lady to get to the school, not after I listened to my son's disappointment all night previously, not after I failed miserably in my personal life, and not after I had to politely and unapologetically request assistance to attend to my personal matters during working hours.

I think the lady was becoming frustrated with me and finally she gave up. There was an older gentleman passing by in the office and she extended her arm and asked him if he can have a look at the application. The only thing that I can think off in my mind is "Dear God you have to let this child get into this school because if he does not Lord knows I have no answers for September, what am I going to tell my son?"

As the old grey haired man begun to peruse my son's application all I could see was his demonstration of checkmarks on a form and I told myself yes this man is looking after my son's application and everything seems to be in order so far. The old grey haired man soon pointed to me and said "Have a seat I will be right back". I saw him disappear down the corridor. I waited for what seemed like an eternity before this man came back, and when he did, he said "Follow me to my office". I humbly took a seat in his office and watched him cross reference all the paperwork until he was finally done. He then said "How do you want to pay; debit or cash?" Once I said debit to him, he said to me "Go to that lady over there and pay the fees".

In my mind I was not sure what was going on but I took a gamble and said "OK I will pay the fees" and I went to the lady and I explained to her that the man in the office sent me to pay the fees. I gave her the paperwork that he gave to me and she processed the payment. Once completed, I went back into his office and he gave me a sheet of paper which was titled "UNIFORMS" and then told me to "Try and get the uniforms before school begins".

Obviously I had a look of bewilderment in my face. This old grey haired man did not advise if my son was accepted into this school, yet he was telling me about the requirements needed for September's school entry and all the appointment dates that I needed to know before my son began his high school in September 2019. Finally, I asked the man "Is my son accepted into your school?" to which he replied "Yes". That was all I needed to know.

My son had a school placement in September 2019 and he was not school-less.

No longer did I feel dejected but I was elated for my son and I was also angry at myself. I was angry at the fact that everything in my life including my work took precedence over my family.

On my drive home I realized that I needed to give my self permission first before I give my permission over to others. As I thought about it more and more, I realized, I needed permission first to be myself, then I needed permission from my self to be a wife to someone, thirdly I needed permission from my self to be a mother to my kids, fourthly I needed to give my self permission to be an employee of a company and fifthly I needed to give my self permission to be a person in this world.

Everything that I thought about on my drive home kept circling back to the fact that I was extremely busy and preoccupied with my work life and the everyday shenanigans of my personal and family life that I did not have time to give my self permission to breathe and be who I am.

I realized quickly, if I do not know who I truly am, if I do not give my self permission first, I am of no benefit to others who are in my life, be in it my work life or my professional life.

I was extremely busy pleasing everyone, that I lost my self in the process of pleasing and I also neglected my part as a mother to ensure that my kids took precedence over my work.

"Having POWER often means saying No."

It was a hard place to be in mentally and slowly I realized that work and employment will always be there, my kids and my family will not be around forever. The time that we as a family now spend and have spent together is extremely precious and the time I spend with my self is more precious and priceless than anything or anyone else.

I needed to give my self permission to be me. I desperately needed to give my self permission to be the true person I wanted to be and not be who everyone else wanted me to be.

It took a wake-up call of realizing, my lack of commitment to my family and my over commitment to my work, almost ended my son's high school dream, even before it started.

Tired of and exhausted from all of this, I finally realized that I came first, without me there is no glue that holds my family together. Just like without food there is no health, without air to breathe there will be no me one day, I will die. I firmly believe, had I continued on that obsessive self-destructive work path, I would have exhausted myself to the point that I am no longer good to myself or anyone else.

This is the main reason why I need to give my self permission to breathe, to eat, to inhale fresh air, to take a break, to smile every day, to enjoy life and to look after myself and my family.

If I do not give my self permission to be who I am or who I was truly meant to be, I will never ever be the best that I can be in this world.

I need to give my self permission first, I need to ask my self for permission, I need to say to my self, "I am giving you permission to be who you want to be". I have to look my self in the mirror and make sure I fully understand that I am giving my self permission to be who I need to be; permission is the most powerful request in this world.

Having permission means acknowledging that you need to give yourself permission to be who you were truly meant to be. Do not wait for someone else to give you permission to be who you are or who you were meant to be.

I waited to ask for permission from my self, I waited until the very last minute when I realized that I was fulfilling everyone else's need except my own need. Once I understood what I was doing, I decided that I will put my self first and give my self permission to be, that which I was destined to be.

This is the most powerful affirmative statement I make every day:

"I give my self permission to be who I am truly meant to be."

Give yourself permission to grieve when there is a loss in your family. Forget what everyone says, you are the only one who knows your pain inside, give yourself time and permission to grieve the way that you are supposed to grieve until you have reached the end of your grief. By grieving you will know yourself, you will rediscover yourself and your happiness will radiate from inside of you.

Give yourself permission to smile every day. Smile amongst all the negativity of the world and amongst all the negativity of your current world.

Give yourself permission to lift your head high and walk as a powerful woman in this world. Women are subjected to a world of injustices, inequality, misfortune, abuse, disrespect, unfairness and negativity.

Women are destined by society to fail even before they are born. Give yourself permission to accept the fact that you are a woman and you are a strong woman who will overcome every burden that is thrown towards you. Never ever let someone put you down. Do not ever let someone's words hurt you and destroy you.

Give yourself permission and the power to walk powerfully, upright, strong and away from negative. Do not let anyone steal the power that you possess inside.

This innate power gives you the ability to give yourself permission to breathe again, to smile again, to laugh again, to live again, to walk again, to talk again and to be who you were truly meant to be again.

Do not let anyone steal your power away from you. Walk with your head held high in your own power.

"Remove yourself from that dirty water you continue to stand in, others are no longer willing to join you in the dirty water you relish in, relocate yourself to the clean water awaiting you and watch your life flourish."
Cindy Bahadur-Ramkumar

Walking in the Power of True Purpose

Walking in my power of true purpose. It is sometimes very difficult for me to differentiate between power and purpose. I have read many books and listened to many learnt educated speakers and educators talk about finding your purpose, finding your true purpose, discovering you and finding everything about your purpose. While I completely agree that I need to find my purpose, I am a strong believer that without power, without my own self power, I will never find my true power and true purpose.

Many struggle with understanding the meaning of purpose. Finding your purpose means being able to live a fulfilled life doing exactly what you love to do, and doing it with so much flavour and passion that you truly and totally enjoy every moment, every second and every minute of doing what you love to do. You will find joy in doing what you love once you find your true power and true purpose.

Finding your purpose also means that you have the ability to suddenly take on the world and introduce others to your world and your method of thinking. Many times I have read, if you do not live a life of purpose, you cannot and are not living a life. I relish these statements because I feel that you really cannot live a life of purpose, if you do not believe that you possess the innate power to live your life of purpose.

"When you come in to your TRUE POWER, you look at the world through different eyes, you become connected to the TRUE you".

It is very tricky and very deceiving to listen to someone who preaches from a podium; this is my purpose, this is what I was meant to do, this is what I was born to do. It is all good and well to understand your true purpose and what you were meant to do but if you truly do not understand how to achieve what you were meant to do then you are not walking in the power of your true purpose.

I firmly believe that everything we do in this life, we need to have the power and the willpower to get it done. If we have to achieve our true purpose, we need firstly to garner the willpower to begin the steps and processes to achieving our true purpose through power.

I believe without power there is no purpose. Without power there is nothing in this life. Without power you cannot and

12

will not attain anything in life be it tangible or intangible. Finally without power there is absolutely no way you can actually achieve your true purpose. Your true purpose comes from your power inside of you. It comes from your innate power to believe that you are able to achieve, create, believe and have the drive to attain your true purpose.

For me, I have tried many times to find my true purpose and to figure out my true purpose. There were and are many days when I lack purpose, cannot find my purpose and I begin to question my very existence.

In this world, I also question the reason for living, the reason that we are put on this earth, the reason we strive to accumulate material possessions constantly and leave everything behind, and I question really what is my true purpose.

I have not found an answer to my true purpose because with every day passing and with every new endeavour my purpose is changing, my true purpose is evolving, my true purpose is being fine-tuned and my true purpose is being redefined.

To advise I have found my true purpose is false and misleading. I am no different from another person walking the street. Just like they are rediscovering themselves and searching internally to discover who they are, I am also trying to find my direction and true purpose. In my mind there lies thousands of ideas, all buzzing around, all with the same outcome and common goal of helping me realize a part of my true purpose.

My true purpose is evolving every day. Some days I feel that my purpose is to help the world, on other days I feel that my purpose is to share my brain, knowledge, and blessings with and on other days I feel that my purpose of existence is bigger than life, bigger than who I am currently, bigger than anyone can believe.

I know that I have the power within me to find my true purpose. This power within me is extremely powerful and I find myself purposefully driven to use the power that I was blessed with to create the purpose that was meant to be for me.

I can never under estimate the true power that I possess for my true intended purpose. Having true power means I have the ability to capitalize on my strengths, enhance my abilities, learn from my past, create my future and live and relish in my now.

The power of my purpose is extremely powerful and sometimes can become overwhelming. My purpose, even though it is not fully defined and I may never be able to fully define it, will continue to evolve daily, however the power that I possess inside of me to achieve my true purpose should never be underestimated. My power inside of me pushes me forward to constantly look from within, to self-develop and to create, while I continue on this journey of life.

There are days when I know I am walking slowly in the power of my purpose and there are days when I know that my power within is slowly dying and I need to pick myself up and move forward again.

Having the innate power within is like having a living breathing entity inside of me. It fuels my purpose and allows me to hone in and enhance my true purpose. Finding and living my true purpose cannot be sustained without walking in the power that I possess within.

"You are truly powerful when you are connected to who you really are."

My biggest challenge was trying to figure out how to extract and enhance my power before beginning to realize my true purpose. Once I figured out how to become more powerful from within, I began to slowly weed out the non-necessary, non-contributory, non-value added items and people from my life. I came to the realization that I gave or I was giving away all my power to things, people, situations and items that added little or no value to my purpose.

For me, the easiest path to walk in my power of true purpose is to remove anything and anyone that has and had a negative impact on me, and blocked me from achieving my full true purpose.

Once I removed all the negativity and negative vibrations

from my life, my true purpose began to reveal itself. No longer was I giving away my power but rather I was taking control of my power to enhance my true purpose.

I can say with utmost clarity that I am truly walking in the power of my true purpose.

"Self-realization comes when you realize that no one else is willing to join you in your pity party. Stop feeling sorry for yourself, pick yourself up and move forward."
Cindy Bahadur-Ramkumar

Walking in the Power of Positivity and Being Positive

During my workday I find myself surrounded by many negative people or people who have negative comments, negative feelings, feelings of anger, dislike, animosity, hatred lack luster for life.

I have to constantly remind myself that I do not want to be surrounded by these people who emit negative energies, negative vibes, and negative vibrations. Persons who possess these type of negative vibrations tend to spoil or dirty the positive energy around me.

I am by nature a very optimistic person and by sheer nature I attract positivity and positive energy towards me. When I am surrounded in the workplace and places of work by negative vibrations and negative energy, my personal aura gets pulled down and makes me feel sad and uncomfortable and sometimes even angry and lost inside.

My entire being relies on positivity and positive vibrations. My internal being and soul always collect and suck up all the positive vibrations around me.

I need to be and remain positive in a negative environment.

My inner being repulses negativity and stays away from it.

I crave and strive to walk in the power of my positivity by changing conversations to a positive, walking away from negative people and not indulging myself in negative talk, negative feedback and negative vibrations.

I enhance my positivity by being upbeat internally and externally and I challenge myself mentally to put a positive spin on a negative situation or put a positive spin in an uncomfortable environment. I try to ensure that there is always a positive influence in the environment I am in and that I consciously search for the positive in every negative environment I find myself into.

"Tap into your True Personal POWER and watch your POWER grow."

It is very tough to convert a negative into a positive. It is even tougher to walk in the power of positivity, and in the power of my positivity when the environment and the atmosphere all around me is contagiously negative.

However, I hold dearly to my heart positive vibrations and I walk in my power of positivity. I make sure that parties to my conversation are not given the ability to destroy my positivity with their negativity. I hold my power of positivity close to my heart. Therefore ensuring I am not able to give it away to anyone.

Negativity depletes my energy every time I am forced to remain positive in a negative environment. There are days when I feel sorry for myself, get angry with myself and sometimes become angry with the person(s) I come into contact with because their negativity and their negative energy consumes my positivity and drains me mentally.

Whenever I get to this negative mental and emotional state, I remind myself that I have to remain positive, that I do not want negative energy to come into my being and I do not want negative or evil to overtake my aura. I remind myself to breathe, and I take long deep breaths to reposition my mind positively.

When I hit that bottomless pit mentally, where I feel I have fallen of the positive bandwagon, I mentally prepare and re-condition myself to force my mind to be grateful for the simplest things that I am blessed with. I put on my appreciation hat and appreciate everything that I am blessed with in my life.

I remind myself daily that life can always be worse than it currently is and that I have lived that worst part of my life already. I make a decision that I am not going to allow anyone to steal my positive, to steal my joy, to steal my freedom, to steal my thought processes and to steal my mind.

I am not going to allow anyone to come into my mind. I am

not going to allow anyone to steal the peace and calm that I have within my mind and my inner being. I am going to lift my head and keep walking forward. I will not look back because the only vibrations that I need in my life are the vibrations of positivity and forwardness.

No other vibrations are needed in my life except positivity and forwardness. There are no other vibrations that I want entered into my being, or want to allow into my personal space besides positivity.

I often have to remind myself of the halo ring around my being. I see similarities to my teachings that I conduct with forklift drivers and maintaining my halo. In this training, I remind drivers of the need to ensure that pedestrians do not get close to their forklift truck thereby preventing an accident or injury, therefore they have to maintain a five feet circular distance around their truck. I labelled this circular distance "a halo". This halo protects the driver and the pedestrian employee from unintended injury.

My halo, my positive halo, my positivity halo, is the five feet halo that I keep around myself and I do not allow any negative vibrations to enter into my space. I do not allow anyone to come into my halo with their negative vibrations. I relocate myself and move my halo if I feel there are others encroaching negatively into my space.

If someone is coming towards me or having a conversation that is negative in nature, I intentionally curtail the conversation by saying that I am busy, I have a phone call to take, I have a meeting to attend to or I have things to complete, or things which needs my attention. In that way,

I protect my halo and avoid my halo from becoming contaminated with negative energy.

My husband always jokes with me because I equate negative energy to the contamination of self. I fully believe that as humans, we do not set out to contaminate and expose ourselves to any form of negative energy contamination. However negative contamination will always exist and seem to find a way to disturb positive vibrations.

In the workplace we normally make a conscious decision not to expose ourselves to any type of infectious chemical contamination due to the risks involved in chemical exposure. However, in our personal lives and with our personal space, we do not make a conscious decision to protect ourselves from the contamination of negativity by others. We do not put any energy into stopping our bodies, beings and lives from being contaminated by negativity.

We do not put energy into purifying ourselves with positivity. While we believe we need to protect ourselves from the dangerous exposures of the world, we do not believe that we need to protect ourselves from negativity and from the persons who possess negative vibrations or are negative in nature. We do not believe that the negative vibrations of others contaminate our inner space and we definitely do not believe we need to protect our inner beings from the dangerous negative vibrations emitted by others.

It is my belief that my power belongs to me and no one

else. My power of thinking positively lies and lives within me. I have made that conscious decision to walk in the power of positivity and to keep my internal and inner being positive at all times. I have made the decision not to allow others to contaminate my space with their negativity and I have made the conscious decision that only I hold the power of positivity in my life.

"Your true POWER comes from within, do not be fooled by others telling you your POWER comes from them or your dependence on them."
Cindy Bahadur-Ramkumar

Walking in the Power of the Present, of the Now

Growing up, as a child I have always been told about the now, about doing things now, about living in the present, about moving on, about making the now and the present the most important time in my life.

I remember many times my parents would say to me that the past is gone leave it alone and the future is very uncertain, all you have is your now. I did not quite get it, and I still have not gotten it until recently, in 2019, when I learnt I had to let go of my past in order for my now and for my future to take place.

I guess for me, I feel like I am a sucker for punishment and somehow it feels like discretely I enjoy the ride of punishment. No matter how many times I remind myself and I condition my mind that I have to let go of the past, I knowingly re-live the past each and every day causing extreme discomfort and mental pain to myself daily.

WALKING IN MY TRUE POWER

I believe, my behaviours from the past demonstrate that I am a glutton for punishment and only until recently I have been able to let go of my past. I always punished myself mercilessly for my past mistakes and the past mistakes of others. Life is interesting, when you really sit down and think of life in perspective, it can either be very difficult or it can be very easy.

We as humans make life very difficult for ourselves. We have a choice every day, and almost on all occasions as humans we always choose the uphill battle rather than the downhill battle. We are always going into battle every day of our lives knowing that the outcome will not be good and that we will end up in tears yet we choose to go into battle (uphill battle). The ability to walk away and not give any thoughts to the discomfort around you is the downhill battle.

This was me. Every day, I consciously and willingly choose to go into battle because I wanted to, I had to prove something to myself, and I had to make the other party's action seem less significant and less important (uphill battle). At the end of my daily battles, to be honest I learnt nothing. I cried more than ever. I was always hurt. I knew the outcome each and every time I went into battle. Yet I continued to battle daily, as internally I was looking for some sort of gratification which I knew I could never find and I would never find and I will never have answers to.

I kept fighting my past believing the more I fought the easier the answer will come to me and that there would be some type of answer. To my disappointment each and every day there were no answers, there were no resolutions, there were no end results, and the only person left hurting was myself.

In December 2019, after ten long years of fighting demons and battles and not winning any, I finally realized that my past will always be my past and that my future will always be undecided and the only time that ever mattered to me was my present, and it was my now.

I have no clear cut answer as to why I had put myself through many years of mental torture, and I have no reason or justifications for any of my past actions. What I do know now is that my present time and my now time is the only time that I have. I have learnt the art of living in the present, living in the now, taking care of myself now, loving myself now, and being the best that I can be now.

"To test a person's character, give them POWER."

I never realized that I was stealing from my now. I lived in my past and was always cheating my future. I would take my now moments and make my now moments miserable, tearful and argumentative. I never realized how important my now was until I learnt the art of appreciating my current moment.

Since I acquired the ability to learn and appreciate my now, I am in a happier place. I live for my now rather than live because of my past and I do not live for my future. I have learnt the art of appreciating my now and understanding my value in my now, I understand and know there is value in the now, value in my now.

I live for my now, I live for the present and I savor every moment of my now. My now makes me happy, my now breathes life into me and my now allows me to capture and appreciate my present moment.

I learnt only I have power over my now. I learnt I cannot change my past, and I have no control over my future, however I have control over my present and I have control over how I want to feel in my present.

Since I found my now and my present, I am no longer worried about my past. I no longer think about my past and I no longer allow my past to be my present. My past stole my present and I have reclaimed my present from my past.

I live for my now, and my present. I live for my current moment. I enjoy every moment of my now. I live each day as if there is no tomorrow, as if it is my last. I live without regrets. I have dreams and plans for my future, and I allow my now to mould my future. I am no longer hung up on my past, my past mistakes and the people who have done me wrong in my past.

My life is no longer about people and their injustices, their selfishness, their greed and their destructive nature, but my life is about me and me being the best me I can be in every now moment of every day.

"Always remind yourself that no one can love you like you love yourself. Learn to love yourself selfishly and watch your life flourish."
Cindy Bahadur-Ramkumar

Walking in my Power of Making a Decision

The most difficult task a person has to make in their life is to make a choice or to choose. Options are always present and a choice always has to be made.

Often, many times we are placed in very uncomfortable situations, amongst groups of many people, in teams where we are not comfortable or even amongst others we are only tolerating for the sake achieving a common goal.

Human nature and aptitude requires that we sit and be quiet, have focus, tolerate, buy time, and not have an opinion. It is very difficult to live in the world where we have many choices and no voice to express our choices.

All the time, circumstances and situations dictates the manner in which we behave. For example, there are many times I am invited to meetings which I know to myself the meetings have no value or little value to my human existence, however because out of sheer necessity or need to attend the meeting and be present, I am crippled to attend and to tolerate the meeting and its attendees. Had I felt the need to respect the fact that I do have a choice, to attend or not attend, I would have refused attendance to meetings many times.

Until today, I never felt I had the power to make a choice, the power to determine which path I would take, the power to decipher my choices and my consequences and the power to stand by my choice. I know I had choices and I always made choices, I just never knew I had the power to make choices and that there was power in making choices.

After much trepidation, I realize having the ability to choose, is only one part of the equation, however having the power to make a choice is even more valuable and important. I realized that I have the power to choose, I have the ability to determine the outcome which I desire.

It took me quite a long time to understand the power that I possess within me throughout my life. I always felt that I was going through the motions. I felt that I was fulfilling the needs of others while the needs of myself became neglected and took a back seat.

I always understood that sitting in a meeting for three hours, was a total waste of my time and added no value to my life. I also understood that I had the power to make a choice to walk out of that meeting because it added no value to me or my scope of business.

"Mastering you is your TRUE POWER."

Counting the number of man-hours that I have spent in meetings throughout my life, I feel that I may have spent at least three to four years of my life wasted behind closed doors enclosed in a room, with persons who added zero value to my life.

If I add those meetings together for twenty years of my working life, I would have attended at least fifteen thousand, two hundred and twenty meetings. I shudder to think how much of my life has been wasted on senseless non-value added, non-productive meetings. In my professional life, even though I was given the right to choose, I never really had the right to make a decision and have a choice. I never fully understood that having the ability to choose, having the ability to say yes or no, having the ability to make a choice, having the ability to make myself happy, all meant that I was giving power to myself.

I realized I was giving away my power to the person in charge of the meeting and the person in charge of the meeting was making all the decisions on my behalf because my voice was often silent and muted in long winding meetings.

I also realized that the main purpose of hosting a meeting was because one person had an opinion and that person wanted to have the entire team go along with and commit to their opinion. It was never a matter of choice but rather a matter of compliance. I realized later in the game, I have the power to choose and I have the power to make a decision to attend to or not to.

"Give people POWER to control their own destiny."

With my power to choose wisely, it gave me the ability to free myself from the bondages of life, free myself from situations, people, environments and meetings.

The power to choose is extremely fascinating to me. Every day, every second of every day and every minute of every day, choices in life are presented to us. We often give up our ability to choose by giving away the power to the person who has forced us to make a decision.

We never realized that during the course of our day, every time we made a decision or made a choice, it allowed us to enter into a different path. For example, when I wake up in the morning, I have a choice to take my alarm clock off or to get up (because my alarm clock went off) and to proceed on with my day. When I give my alarm clock the power to allow me to sleep extra, I have given away my power to the alarm clock, whereby the alarm clock would wake me up at a different time. Alternately had I immediately awaken when the alarm clock goes off, I demonstrate to myself I have taken control of that power of choice.

When I go into my closet in the morning I make a decision to choose what I want to wear for the day. The choice from my decision dictates my mood for the entire day. I have given my mind the power to choose the way that I want to feel for the entire day. If I take away that power of choice from my mind, I then allow myself to feel the way that I want to feel.

On days when I do not feel perky and nice, my mood is reflected in my clothing of choice, and my clothing worn emanates a feeling of not pretty and not nice. On days when I want to feel professional, sophisticated and exquisite, I choose clothing that allows me to feel that way.

On my way into the office, I make choices. Every choice that I make has an outcome, either negative or positive. For example, if I take route number one, it will get me to my ending destination but it will cost me twenty-five dollars in gas, one and a half hours in time and a certain level of frustration when driving in traffic. If I choose route number two, it will cost me fifteen dollars in toll fees, takes me to my destination in ten minutes, it alleviates the pain of being stuck in traffic, but there is a financial cost associated with taking the route.

Choices made in selecting my travel routes dictates the manner, method and comfort in which I spend and value my time. At that point in time when I make a decision to take a specific route I have decided that I have the power to choose the route that will make me happy. At that point in time when I decided that I am not comfortable with a choice but I continue on with that choice, my power of choice and clarity is taken away from me.

There is power in my choice to awake every morning or to sleep extra. There is power in my choice to attend meetings or not. There is power in my choice to choose the clothes I wear, which sets my mood for the day, and there is power in choice to choose the routes that I travel daily.

I have given full control of my power to my choice rather than have the full power to choose, I make a choice and delight in making choices. The power to choose is the most powerful aspect of the power that we possess. Every choice that we make has an outcome. The outcome determines our mood levels; happiness, sadness, irritability, angriness, anger and possibly hatred. Inside each of us, we all have the power to choose, we just need to know how to find our power within and how to utilize that power for the benefit of ourselves and not for the benefit of others.

We have to be selfish in our choice, selfish in the manner in which we use our power to choose.

If we approach each day in this life as the only and most valuable day that we have in this world, we will realize that the choices we make for that day will always be the choices that we want to make, rather than the choices that are imposed upon us. If we understand that with every choice there is a mood that aligns with it, we will most definitely always make the right choice, and we will at all times ensure that we utilize our power to choose the right way, the right method, the right road, the right job, the right deal, the right meeting, the right decision, the right home and the right comfort.

We will, at all times, make the right choice in the best interest of ourselves, fully understanding the power that we possess inside of us allows us to make choices only in our best interest.

There is power in choice. Once I realized that there is power in choice, I now choose wisely. I intentionally choose my outcomes.

"Your past is gone, your future is uncertain, your now holds the most value, make your life as valuable and as worthy as you require it to be."
Cindy Bahadur-Ramkumar

Walking in the Power of NO

For as long as I can remember, from the onset of being a child, to being a teenager, to being an adult, I was always told that you should never say no to anyone and that you should always try to help, that you should always extend a hand and that you should, if you could, assist as much as you can.

As I get older, I am realizing that everything I learnt and I did, I did it out of respect to not say no. I now have to unlearn my past as an adult and begin saying no. I now realize there is power in saying the words no. I do not have to say yes if I do not want to say yes rather a simple no is sufficient. I do not need to justify or give an explanation why I am saying no, no explanation needed.

I know now, that in the past, where even though I was uncomfortable with a task I would agree to do it only because I did not want the other party to be displeased, offended or unhappy. So at all times, against all odds, with my best judgment, and even though I did not want to, I always said yes. Because, yes, being the operative word, was always the best and only response that should be given.

I realized later on in life that I acquired something, I acquired a disease unknown to me. This disease was the disease to please. This disease was a disease to say yes at all times. It was a disease to not say no even though every part of me wanted to say no.

I lived all my life, in fact every day and every part of my life pleasing everyone. I think I found my culmination and climax when I did not have it inside of me anymore to please anyone. I was mentally, emotionally and physically exhausted. I realized that saying no was my only option.

I am not an expert at saying no, however I have acquired the ability to say no, and slowly but surely one day I will become an expert at saying no.

One night I realized that I had to put a stop to this disease to please, a disease that was taking me over, a disease that was taking over my free time, a disease that took my free time away from my kids and myself, a disease that was consuming me, a disease that was killing me inside.

In the workplace, I believed had an insatiable desire to please. It was born out of a desire to not say no. I did not know how to not say no. Whenever I was asked to do a task even though it did not pertain to me, or it had no relevance to me, or the work that I was doing, I never said no to the request to assist, it did not matter what it was, I was always picking up additional projects, managing extra tasks, spearheading deals etc., I was being me, helpful and always giving.

When I said yes to a task, I realized I was doing a task the majority of my other co-workers did not want to do or had no interest in doing. My inability to say no stole away me from me and stole my personal time away from me. This stealing of my time was as a result of me not being able to say no.

Because of these agreed commitments, there were many days, when during my lunch hour I never took lunch, or I never had a break time or even took a break. While I appreciated that my work day went extremely fast, I would kick myself mentally by saying "I did not get time to pay my bills or I did not get time to write a chapter in my book or I did not get time to make a phone call" and each and every day my work day was like this.

"Your truth will set you free, it is your birth given right to speak the truth."

I was consumed by the disease to please or the disease to say yes. I never knew what the word "no" meant or was, and I never knew how to say no, or never could bring myself to say no to a request.

My rude awakening came a Friday night, closer to the end

of August 2019. I had just gotten home about 6.00 p.m. and was asked to complete some confidential paperwork for someone. I loved what I do, and I know that I have acquired the ability to perfect certain tasks and complete it quickly. It was easier and faster to complete by myself for this person rather than the person spending hours and hours completing it.

When I followed up with the person I was completing the task for, free of charge of course, because I was providing assistance to her out of the goodness of my heart, out of my ability to not say no, out of care and compassion, I called the person and the person was at a club and restaurant, out partying. I was shocked. My mind reminded me how stupid I was. I was sitting at home, on a Friday night, completing paperwork on a computer, which took three hours to complete, for someone who was out partying and having a good time elsewhere.

That night I realized that I had to put a stop to this disease to please. A disease that was taking me over. This disease to say yes was consuming all my free time. This disease was stealing my free time away from my kids and my family, this disease was stealing me from me.

My heart broke into a million pieces knowing that I was sitting behind a computer for three hours, doing work for someone else, because they did not see the need to do it themselves, or they did not want to complete it themselves, and I was giving up my personal time because I did not have the ability to say no when asked to complete it.

Slowly I began to master the art of saying no, or saying I do not have time, or saying not at this current moment. I have not perfected it, but I have mastered the art of saying no, the "say not at this current moment" to everyone.

I now understand that there is power in saying no and that the power solely belongs to me. I am reclaiming my free time from others and giving myself more free time and more power to say no.

"Living life does not mean you have to agree on everything, it is ok to express your opinion. There is POWER in honesty."
Cindy Bahadur-Ramkumar

Walking in the Power of Clarity

There is power in clarity. Clarity is defined as being clear, precise, concise, and having focus. Having clarity means that you are able to achieve with preciseness and precision anything you set your mind to achieve.

Prior to clarity, there is always confusion. There are always many choices to be made and many decisions to be made with varying and multiple outcomes. Having clarity gives focus and gives you the ability to go after what you love, what you are passionate about and what you want.

For example, an entrepreneur, by my definition, is a person who has many, many business ideas, who has many thoughts about business, who seems to know the next best thing, next best invention, next best idea all the time. However the entrepreneur is always unable to bring his/her ideas to fruition because there is no clarity in any of the ideas. There are lots of verbiage in his/her ideas but no clarity.

An entrepreneur's mind is an extremely busy mind, it is a

mind without clarity and focus.

With clarity comes focus. If an entrepreneur can focus on just one idea and take it to fruition, the entrepreneur would be immensely successful. If an entrepreneur can have clarity in terms of the preciseness of the idea, that entrepreneur will be successful.

"Live life as if you know where you are going, you arrived where you were meant to be and you belong where you ought to be."

Clarity means being clear and precise, in thought and action. For example, while driving along a long winding road, without clarity, a junction road appears, bewildered and confused we would choose any turn, left or right because we believe it is the best turn and hope for the best possible outcome.

On the other hand if we are driving along that road with intense clarity, even prior to starting, we know our meeting point, when we arrive at the junction road, there would be zero hesitation to choose a path, because we already know where we are going and how to get to our intended destination.

Clarity reduces frustration, brings unfocused ideas to the

forefront with more focus and ensures the intended outcome is achieved.

Clarity breeds simplicity. Having clarity makes life less complicated and allows for ease of understanding and undertaking. For example, I have a project that has a deadline date fast approaching, I am working on the project tirelessly with a great amount of anxiety and anticipation. I also have a heightened sense of frustration, stress and confusion because the deadline seems to be fast approaching.

Without clarity, I would stress myself out uncontrollably to the point of a close mental breakdown. With clarity, my frustration will be reduced or eliminated, I am no longer anxious, I maintain composure and keep a steady pace, I focus on the tasks at hand and I am able to meet and exceed my deadlines and timelines.

I myself did not understand clarity and its full meaning until after many trial and errors. Life had taken me on and pulled me under. I was consumed by the demands of life, the demands of being a mom, of being a wife, of being a working woman and I was being buried alive in my mind.

One day, I was alone in my thoughts when the word clarity kept popping into my mind. I did not know what that word meant and what I was supposed to do with that word. The word kept popping into my mind and into my conversations with others.

"Clarity, you need clarity", my mind kept replaying. The

more I replayed it, the more I began to understand what it meant. It meant that I needed to be clear and focused on one task only and not on a million tasks at once. But more importantly, it meant that I needed to figure out what I wanted to do with my life and figure it out quickly with clear focus, and preciseness. It also meant that there was little or no self-doubt in my mind about what I needed to do with my life.

My mind was taking me to a million different places and directions all at once. Clarity kept me grounded and focused on what I needed to do to become me.

Had these words "clarity, you need clarity" not popped into my mind, I am one hundred percent sure that I would be dabbling in a million tasks and never mastering any.

There is power in clarity. There is focus in having clarity. There is resilience in having clarity and there is discipline in having clarity.

Having clarity gave me a new chance at life. It gave me a new meaning to live again. It gave me a new purpose and it reignited the old purpose within me which was buried somewhere, desperately trying to get out.

The acquisition of my newly found power of clarity, meant there was no stopping me. Every task that I undertook, I approached it with a certain level of precision and preciseness. I approached it as a process; with a beginning, a middle and an end in mind.

Every thought I thought, I began to condition my mind to think with clarity. If the thought was not clear, I decided that I was not going to entertain it in my mind. I began to train my mind to move on to the next thought if the existing thought was not clear or precise.

Every conversation I had with others, if the conversation was futile, I either tuned my mind out of the conversation, I stopped the conversation or I excused myself out of the conversation. If the conversation was not clear, and there was no focus or thought, and there was lots of noise and babbling, I made it my duty to find a way to exit that conversation.

I quickly understood that my heart, my soul and my mind was desperate for clarity. When the environment or situation was not clear, I felt I did not belong there, and that there was no value to my time.

Having clarity gave me the power to choose and it gave me the power to seek out value in everything I did and said. Having clarity also thought me to disengage myself from environments and situations that had no added value to me.

Acquiring clarity gave me the power to choose, it gave me the power to decide the outcome of my situations, conversations and feelings. Clarity helped me decide between right, wrong and indifferent.

The power of clarity has made my life increasingly better and has helped me hone in to the skills that I needed to grow and become the person I was destined to become.

I am extremely grateful that the words "clarity, you need clarity" popped into my mind. Without these words, my life would or may still have been in shambles, and I would still be searching for something, not knowing what I was searching for, but remain still searching.

My life was like a dog chasing its tail. The more I kept chasing my life, the more circles I was going around, yet I could never reach my goals. Just like the dog would chase its tail and try to catch up to its tail, the dog continues to go around in circles attempting to catch its tail, after a while the effort of tail catching becomes futile, so to I was going in circles to trying to catch my running away life which became futile after a while because I too was also spinning around in circles.

With clarity, and the power that clarity possesses, I am now in a better position in my life, my life is more defined, my life is lived more on purpose, my life has more structure, less confusion and more discipline.

I realized the more I believed in the power of clarity, and the more I decided I wanted clarity rather than discord in my life, I was hungrier for clarity, hungrier than ever before to achieve that path destined for me.

"The only path to where you truly belong is to be clear in thought."
Cindy Bahadur-Ramkumar

CINDY BAHADUR - RAMKUMAR

Walking in the Power of Food

I never really had to value my heath or a healthy eating lifestyle. I was always of a slimmer built, with a higher metabolism and could have consumed any type or amount of food or desert my heart desired without repercussions or guilt. I enjoyed eating because I never gained weight and because food was awesome to eat.

Over the past five years, I became a stress eater. I ate because I was stressed and needed to divert my attention elsewhere. Initially stress eating did not bother me because there was no change in my physical disposition. However, I slowly began to observe an increase in my weight from one hundred and twelve pounds to one hundred and twenty pounds. I was buying my clothing one size bigger. This did not really bother me that much because I was still skinny. Over a six-month period, I went from a size seven to a size ten. The weight gain bothered me. I was not able to find clothing that fit me anymore.

I bought clothes that were bigger than I was or smaller than I was. The smaller clothes gave me comfort and the bigger clothes gave me hope.

My breaking point came one day when I was in a store, asking for a size ten or twelve and there was none. I rummaged through the racks desperately looking for something that I could fit into. The Sales Associate in a very facetious and bold manner advised me to visit a Plus Size Store, so I can find clothing for my size. At that moment my soul died and went to heaven and my self-image was shattered and tarnished forever. I never felt so humiliated in my life, as I felt that day.

I felt like I was worthless and like there was no hope for me in this world. At that moment my soul died and my body was standing there staring at her in disbelief. After recomposing myself, I politely smiled, said thank you and exited the store.

After that encounter, my lack of care for my health took a downward spiral, and I kept eating food for comfort. I ate everything that was present and available to me. Food became my comfort and source of relief. I was no longer eating for pleasure and enjoyment, I was eating for comfort and relief.

I needed comfort and relief and I needed something to make me feel good. Food was my drug which made me feel good, it was the drug that masked my feelings to the world, it was the drug that allowed me to escape my current reality for another and it was the drug that gave me the assurance that everything was going to be ok.

My life was not ok. My life was in shambles and a huge mess. I was an excellent performer in my own life. I performed well for the public and for everyone to see, but I was hurting inside and I was dying inside.

Food gave me the courage to survive. My painful existence was covered with the pleasures of food. My weight began to rapidly increase and there was no stopping my eating frenzy.

At that moment in my life, food gave me power. It gave me the power to bury myself into my sorrows and into my pitiful life. It gave me the power to embrace each day as a new day, and it gave me the power to mask my life and put on a good show for others.

I did not know the power of food. I did not know the control food had over and on me. I did not know that consuming food could take me to exceptional highs in my life and to lows that are seldom ever spoken about but are very present in my life.

I quickly became a stress eater and a midnight eater. The more I ate, the more I felt I was ok in my world. I actually began to feel that I was safe in my world of food and that no one could touch me. I was relentless in my food pursuit.

My reality though, was quite different. I was quickly outgrowing all my clothing and was constantly purchasing bigger and bigger clothing. My closet became a closet of small clothing on the inside and on the outside of my closet there was a stock area of bigger and bigger clothing. The more clothing I bought, the more I appeared to need. It was a vicious circle that I had gotten myself caught up in and I could not get out of it.

It took me about three years to realize that I had given away my power to food. The day I realized I had given my power away to food was the day I sat in my closet and cried for hours and hours. Prior to sitting in my closet and crying for hours, I struck up a verbal fight with my husband blaming him for my weight gain. I could not find any clothes to fit into and we had an engagement to attend.

"Life only has meaning when we decide to give it meaning."

Each day, before work I would walk into my closet and try on clothes that I knew I could not fit into. Ritually I did this every day, hoping to fit into something to go to work. One morning, I believed my soul exploded. My husband kept making fun of me, in a humorous way, "Eat more and let's see what you can fit into", and I believed those words broke me. Those words were like the straw that broke the camel's back. Those words catapulted my life into tears, shame, embarrassment and humiliation.

The part my husband forgot to include in his words, was he was also a contributory factor amongst many other factors to my internal self-demise. He indirectly forgot to acknowledge his behaviors catapulted my life in an alternate direction.

I did not go to work that day, I worked from home, however I broke down in my closet, for what seemed like eternity. I cried and cried until there were no more tears left, but more importantly I cried because I was feeling sorry for myself and I was in a self-pity mode.

I cried for my life, I cried because of the nasty hand dealt to me in life, I cried because evil people existed in my life and I could not get rid of them and I cried because I was tired and exhausted with life, I cried for everything.

The power of food broke me that day. It broke me to minute and miniscule pieces. It broke me to self-pity and it broke me to become a broken woman once again.

Food also controlled my moods. I was a bitter angry person to myself only. To the world I was smiling and happy, but to myself, I was a bitter angry person. I was bitter and angry inside. I hated who I was becoming and I hated myself when I looked at myself everyday in the mirror.

I was angry at life, with life and with the injustices of the world. I was angry with the food that I ate and continued to relish and delight in. My moods were riding a roller coaster every day. On days when my roller coaster was heading downwards, my moods were taking a downward spiral and I was turning to food for comfort to alleviate my self-pity and bitter moods. On days when my roller-coaster was going upwards, my moods were also going upwards, and I ate more, not out of self-pity but because food was available to eat and it was enjoyable.

The more I ate, the more weight I gained and the more I rode my rollercoaster of moods.

From that day in my closet when I broke down and cried for hours, I made a decision to stop my life from spiraling out of control. I enrolled myself in a gym and I began to see slow and subtle changes in my life. I began to feel good about myself and my food choices.

I was actually losing weight and was beginning to fit into some of my working clothing. I was also making good food choices, knowing the difference between good food and bad food.

I began to educate myself on smart food choices and I began to choose the food I wanted to consume. I was no longer eating out of self-pity but I was eating because I cared about what I wanted to put into my body.

It took me three years to realize that there was power in food. It was a slow, painful and steady realization. Unfortunately, to get to this realization, I spiraled downwards, and had to pick myself up again.

I realized that consuming food was powerful and that it was engulfed with power. I just had to find that right power. I gave away my power to food, I gave my power to food that made me feel good. I never again substituted my power of good feeling for food consumption.

Once I was able to reclaim my power from food my personal life of eating took a drastic change for the better. I was more aware of what I ate and more conscious of what I was putting into my body.

There is power in the food I ate and now eat. I now choose the power I want to hold and consume.

"Never be afraid to be you, the world is eagerly awaiting your presence and entry."
Cindy Bahadur-Ramkumar

Walking in the Power of Good Health

In life we all make choices. Our choices determine our outcomes. I made a choice to bury myself in food, of which the majority was bad food which allowed me and my life to spiral out of control.

I also allowed my health to deteriorate. For a woman in her thirties, my body operated like a body that was sixty and over, but looked like a body of a twenty-five year old.

I was lethargic, lazy, always out of breath, always in pain, complained about everything and had the world of excuses for not wanting to make myself better.

I was the classic example of help the world but not yourself. I helped everyone in the world except myself. I became very lazy and didn't care for my health. Again, if you looked at me, you would never know that I was failing, however inside of me I was failing.

I became an over achiever to the outside world, I was winning awards which meant nothing to me. I was the "Employee of the Year" for a multinational company, I was always the "Employee of the Month", "Best Achiever" etc., but these awards meant nothing to me. I was achieving these awards and milestones with very little effort. While the world applauded my efforts, to me my external efforts meant nothing.

I was miserable inside. I had lost my power a few years aback to food and I had no zeal to change the life that was hiding inside of me.

Like everything else in life, there was a breaking point, and my breaking point was the day I could not walk up my stairs without being out of breath. I would walk a few steps and be completely out of breath. I would go into a meeting a try to catch my breath upon entry into the meeting while having to contribute to the meeting.

I was not overweight or heavyset, I was hovering between one forty-five to one forty-nine pounds. I believe I was putting a lot of stress on my heart. I also believed I found excuses to cover up the fact that I was struggling to breathe and struggling to catch my breath by masking it with focusing on everyone and their needs and everything that needed my attention.

My kids were making fun of me, not maliciously but innocently joking that I was out of breath every time I walked up the stairs.

Every time I walked up my stairs, I needed to take a five-minute break to catch my breath and recuperate before I began another task. It became humiliating after a while, because the innocent jokes kept hitting home to me.

When I made that decision to change my life and become healthier, it was the most powerful health decision I ever made. It was the most powerful decision I made for me and not anyone else. I decided to please me and no one else this time around. This time, my health was about me and no one else. I was about to catapult my life into a whole new direction and I was really excited about it.

"Try POWER thinking, using your POWER to think POWERFUL thoughts."

I began healthy daily rituals which made me feel better and made me happy both from the inside and outside. I was religious with walking every day, I would walk for one to two hours daily, and with everyday walking, I tried something new. I began to run and walk, I even did step climbing and I was enjoying it. I quickly found power in looking after myself and I found joy in everything that I was doing for myself to make myself happy.

I realized quickly that there was power in good health and I was hungry to attain that power. Walking got me excited, it was no longer about losing weight, but it was about being outside, enjoying the fresh air, taking my mind away from the world and ultimately seeing the benefits reflected in the improvement of my health.

I could walk without feeling breathless, I could go up and down my stairs and no longer be ashamed because I was no longer out of breath, and most importantly I was happy. The power of good health brought me happiness inside, a kind of happiness that I was seeking and did not know how to find.

With every daily walk, I challenged myself to go a bit further, I pushed myself a bit harder and I relished in the good feeling of the power I possessed inside of me to strive to be healthy.

I was making good food choices, not because of the food I wanted to eat, but because of the food I needed to live by and the feeling good food gave me inside.

I kept reminding myself of two things; my body is my temple and I get to choose what I wanted to allow into my temple and secondly, my body is like a car, if I put tainted gasoline into it, it will not perform at its optimal and it will stutter and choke on its drive, if I put good gasoline into it, it will perform at its optimal, even outperforming itself, my body needed good food only.

I began to realize that I wanted my temple to be clean and wholesome and I wanted my car (body) to perform beyond its optimal performance. I was making a conscious decision to allow only good food into my body, but more importantly I was making that conscious decision to breathe again, to walk again, to climb those stairs again and to not be breathless and out of breath.

On my most breathless moments I realized there was power in health, and more power in good health with good food.

Once I understood that there was power in good health, I was hungry for more power and even hungry for more good health every day. I was happier inside and more contented with myself.

I found joy in being healthy and in maintaining a healthier lifestyle. I found more joy in deciding what I wanted to put into my mouth and my body and I found even more joy in living again.

I found joy in being me and who I was supposed to be and I found joy in choosing to give my power to my health and giving my power to my life.

"Always make you happy, your happiness should never be dependent on someone else's approval of you."
Cindy Bahadur-Ramkumar

Walking in the Power of Fear

Fear cripples the mind and directly cripples a person from moving forward in life. Fear is often masked as fear of the unknown, fear of not knowing what is next, fear of just being afraid and fear of unintended or intended outcomes.

I never quite understood why I was afraid to undertake certain tasks or make certain decisions, however I kept delaying decisions until the inevitable and when the time was up and I was forced to make a decision.

I always knew inside of me I was afraid. Not quite sure why I was afraid or what I was afraid of, however over time I realized I was afraid of the unknown outcome. I was afraid of the negative outcome and the failure perceived with the outcome.

Fear had the ability to control my power and it always did. I was afraid to make decisions, I was fearful of outcomes and always hesitant to "jump" and hesitant to take the next step.

With time, I realized that my fear of the unknown was crippling me and that I was miserable inside my own brain, because I could not and would not make a decision and move on. I felt like me delaying my decision was allowing me to relax in my known and avoid the inevitable of the unknown.

Once I realized that I was always sitting on the fence and I was labelled as a fence surfer, I decided to jump. I began to take chances and live with the outcomes.

I noticed my husband was also afraid of making decisions. I noticed that he would abdicate his husbandly decisions to me because he himself was afraid to commit to something.

Fear of the unknown indirectly controlled our lives, silently, unknowingly and knowingly. The more fear that I possessed inside, the longer I took to make a decision or arrive at a resolution and the non-resolution festered inside of me longer than ever.

I am still not quite sure why I am afraid to make quick in-the-moment decisions, but I know I am not afraid to make calculated thought out decisions. Maybe my fear was born out of part of my childhood, or maybe out of observing others in the world or in the workplace, I am not quite sure and I cannot pinpoint one particular situation which leads me to the answer.

Once I started making decisions, and living with the outcomes, I realized that making spur-of-the-moment decisions was not as bad as my mind perceived it to be. I also realized that the power of my mind was crippling my future endeavors. Slowly, I realized that my mind was holding my power of fear and my mind was pushing me to be fearful of life and everything in it.

I realized quickly that my thoughts in my mind were not visible and never will be visible to anyone else. So in reality, it did not matter what I thought, no one knew anyway.

My fear of undertaking any task, or making a decision was crippled by the thoughts in my mind. The thoughts in my mind, were stealing my power to think rationally and my power of certainty away from me, hence making me afraid and fearful.

The concept of fear, although known to me, was subdued and unknown in my vocabulary. As humans we never admit or acknowledge that we are afraid. Society has taught us that fear demonstrated is a sign of weakness, when in reality all fear means is having a lack of ability to make a coherent decision.

"Get hooked on that good feeling of being POWERFUL."

Once I began to embrace fear, I was no longer afraid to make decisions. I directly and indirectly taught myself that there will always be two outcomes to every decision. A likely outcome and an unlikely outcome. A likely outcome is the intended outcome, the outcome that I was hoping for, and an unlikely outcome is the unintended outcome that I was not hoping for.

Understanding that there are always two outcomes and will always only be two outcomes to every decision and situation I am placed in, made life a bit easier and bit more livable. I now had a plan to move forward. My plan entailed attaining likely outcomes at all times, however in the event that I had attained an unlikely outcome, I was willing to create an alternate plan for the unlikely outcome to make it a likely outcome.

My husband is the epitome of walking in the power of fear. I call him an "excellent fence watcher and fence surfer". A lot of times, I have to keep pushing him to make a decision and move on. I personally think he enjoys the fence watching, fence surfing and worrying himself to death or out of his mind with an outcome which is not even evident, visible or present.

For example, he is afraid of failure, so he refuses to try again, he has a fear of troublesome and burdensome people so he shuts himself down and hides from the world, he is afraid to be who he wants to be, so he buries himself in thoughts of who he believes he should be and the worst of all, he undertakes tasks and jobs that are of no relevance to him or which adds no value to himself because he is afraid of doing that which brings him joy. His innate fear cripples him from moving forward and steals the power he has within him to be the best he can be and be who he was truly mean to be.

If he can understand fear and that there will always be only two outcomes to every situation and decision, his life would be less complicated and less worrisome. He is a work in progress and slowly he is understanding that there is power in everything he does, think and says.

The power of fear is crippling and sometimes disastrous. There is power in fear. The goal should always be to reclaim your power from fear. Face the fear head on and make a decision, with the understanding there will only be two possible outcomes from any decision.

Knowing that there will always be a pleasing outcome and non-pleasing outcome helps in disabling the fear from within and allows you to have more power inside of you to direct to other meaningful things in life.

Reclaim your power from the fear hidden within, use the power that is stolen by fear and direct that power to finding resolutions to the unlikely outcomes.

I define fear as a four letter word with two possible outcomes; a likely and an unlikely outcome. My definition of fear has allowed me to reclaim my power from fear and live my life with more meaning and purpose. I no longer let fear steal my power but I let my power guide me to fear so that I can choose an outcome and move on.

"Be true and honest with yourself, you owe it to you to live your life truthfully and honestly, stop hiding your feelings and fears."
Cindy Bahadur-Ramkumar

Walking in the Power of Self-Treatment

I woke up one morning in July 2019 at a hotel in Myrtle Beach, South Carolina and I could not move my neck in any direction, not up or nor down, neither left nor right. It was the most painful experience ever.

It felt like my neck was frozen and every gesture or movement I made was torturous and traumatizing. I was in tremendous pain and tears were flowing down my face incessantly.

My husband stood by me and was staring at me in disbelief and with surprise as if to remind me through silence stares that he was helpless and felt helpless because I was becoming immobile.

Every part of my neck was in excruciating pain, I could not turn it to the left or right, nor look up or down. If and when I did, it was because I was desperate and needed something, which unfortunately I endured the pain in order to achieve short term success for my family.

My husband graciously volunteered myself and himself to visit a pharmacy a couple of blocks away to purchase some medication. We purchased over-the-counter painkillers and muscle rubs.

Those medications aided in the short term alleviation of the pain and assisted in some pain reduction. I was able to have some semblance of a normal vacation for a few hours, however, the pain free life was short-lived once the medication had run its course and had worn out. My husband continued to rub and massage my neck to alleviate my pain.

"Only you know your TRUE POWER, do not let others tell you otherwise."

My pain scale was a nine out of ten and there was nothing I could have done until I returned to Canada. I had emergency medical insurance, but that was futile to use, I could not find a doctor available to see me. I tolerated the pain for the last two days of vacation.

Upon arrival to the airport in Charleston, South Carolina, I dreaded the flight back to Canada. I really enjoy and delight in travelling, but this flight was the worst I had experienced. It was not the flight or the airplane, it was my heightened pain level and my inability to sit comfortably on the plane. A two hour flight felt like a lifetime of flying. It was the most uncomfortable flight I had in my life. Throughout the entire flight, I kept holding my neck, every tiny move caused an excruciating level of discomfort.

Once we landed at Niagara Falls, New York, I was determined to get out of the USA immediately and return to Canada to seek medical treatment. My husband asked me if I could drive and I said yes, as I preferred to drive, driving allows me to relax and takes me into a world of personal gratification and satisfaction. I really dislike being a passenger.

I decided that I would drive, as long as I utilized both side view mirrors and the rear view mirror, I would be fine. What I did not cater for was the roughness of the roads and the fact that every bump in the road pushed my neck into a frenzy of excruciating pain.

After fifteen minutes of driving, I had to pull aside on the highway and let my husband take over the steering wheel. I found that holding my neck upright and straight brought immense relief, and as such, for one and a half hours I held onto my neck with both arms to obtain some sort of relief and less pain.

Never in my life had I slept sitting up, but that night I did. I had no choice. My neck pain had escalated, and I did not want to be admitted to a hospital, because it was after midnight when we arrived to our home, I took a prescriptive painkiller I had in my medicine cabinet and tolerated the pain, until the morning, after which I checked myself in to my doctor's office.

My doctor prescribed antibiotics because I had an inflamed neck, muscle rub and pain medication. In a matter of one hour after my doctor's visit I was feeling a tremendous amount of relief. I also bought myself a heat pad which I wrapped around my neck and my back to reduce the swelling and inflammation.

I was guilty of not taking care of myself. My body had shown me signs of pain and fatigue previously. I ignored these signs and continued to live my life accordingly. I was forced to visit a massage therapist and a physiotherapist to have someone work on my neck, shoulders, upper and lower back.

Even though I had medical benefits and the full works as it pertains to health benefits, I was lazy to look after myself. I am not sure if lazy is the right choice of words, however I refused to look after my well-being because everyone's well-being in my family always took precedence and was always more important than mines.

I believe, I was just being a mom and a woman. I remembered my mom and dad used to always tell me to "Take care of yourself first". I never adhered to their advice. I took care of everyone else first.

My mom always said "Our bodies are like vehicles, if we do not take care of the car, the parts tend to need lubricants and they break due to wear and tear and lack of lubrication". So to our bodies, if we do not take care of it, it will break at some point in time and will need tremendous amounts of repair to get it working again.

I did not realize there was power in self-treatment. Once I had no choice but to look after my body, I fully realized how much care my body was missing. Sadly, my pain and wear and tear was beyond a few treatments of repair. I needed treatments, at minimum three times a week from July 2019 until January of 2020.

Once the massage therapist began to work on my back, it was unbelievable to imagine the extent of my sore upper back, neck, shoulders and lower back. There were knots everywhere in my muscles and these knots were pulling on my nerves and tendons. I always had headaches emanating from the back of my head, now I know the cause of these headaches were tight and stiff back and neck muscles.

I believe, had I intervened when I had my initial pain, I would have needed possibly one to three massage sessions to alleviate the initial problem. I was too far into my pain, that one to three sessions were useless.

I felt instant gratification when the massage therapist placed his hand onto my back and began to work my muscles. I kept asking myself, why did not I come earlier, why did not I look after myself earlier? I was angry with myself and there was nothing I could have done at that moment to make myself feel better. As I laid there enjoying the painful massage, it was a bitter sweet kind of painful pain. Since July 2019 to January 2020, and as I write this book, I am still continuing my massage therapy sessions, at minimum three times a week.

Losing full neck control was a painful lesson to learn and I am still learning from it. Had I taken care of myself, just like I take care of my car, making sure everything is working well prior to me driving off, I also should have taken care of my body in the same manner. I am learning now to take care of myself. I have enrolled myself in every medical health benefit I can capitalize on at no cost to me, I even went to the extent of enrolling myself in facials, manicures, pedicures and many self-treatment sessions.

Luckily for me the damage was not extensive, but some remedial work is needed. Now every time I lay on that massage table I am appreciative of life and appreciative of the ability to look after myself and remind myself that it could have been worse than it is currently.

I am at a stage in my life, where in a very selfish manner, my new philosophy is "life is about me only". It took me twenty years to realize the very same thing my dad and mom preached to me constantly, which was "to take care of yourself first and everything else will fall into place". Unfortunately, I took care of everyone else, allowing their lives to fall into place and failed to take care of myself, my health and my personal needs.

I understood the power of self-treatment when I was in pain and I needed to take care of myself for myself to feel good. I also understood that treating myself was good, and that being treated was even more powerful.

It was clear to me that the feeling I was missing, was found and it was even more clearer to me that I was taking time to treat myself and to make myself feel good and, that in itself was the most powerful move I could have made for me with my life.

There is nothing more powerful than taking care of yourself and treating yourself to life simple pleasures. There is power in treatment, and more power in self-treatment. I unfortunately learnt the hard way, by a process of excruciating pain and tears that my body was crying out for help. I never heeded my body calls and cries for help. I was too busy and preoccupied with making everyone else's life more livable and pleasurable, that I forgot that my body and my life needed help and care also.

I was very happy that I found my power and even more happier that my power was awaiting my arrival and joined me in my journey of self-treatment.

From the day that I laid on that massage table, in excruciating pain until today's date, March 22nd 2020, I have no regrets about the amount of time and money I have spent on myself. I found that innate willpower inside of me to take care of myself and I found that power inside of me to allow me to take time out from everything and time off for myself, to take care of myself.

Trust me, when I say there is power in self-care, and that taking care of oneself is very powerful. It's an innate feeling inside of you that can never be explained in words, it is a feeling that only the soul and inner being understands and knows fully well. That powerful feeling that I now possess never gets quenched because only now I understand that taking care of myself is the most powerful move ever.

There is power in self-care. I became more mindful of myself and more mindful of the body I am blessed with. I became more insightful into the needs of my soul and I spent more time tending to my inner being and soul needs rather than neglecting my needs for the needs of others.

Strangely though, when I look back on my caring mannerisms, the times when I put my family needs before mines, was not as important as I had imagined or believed in my mind they were. I always thought they needed me around and that taking an hour away from them was detrimental and life changing to them, so I was always there, always around, and never neglecting their needs, even when they did not need me, I was still present, I was always around and I never left their sides.

My family knew I had their back at all times. Now that I began to attend all these self-care sessions for myself out of sheer need, I realized that one hour away from my family was not life changing, that they could live without me for an hour and strangely they never missed my presence for that hour.

In fact there are many times I attended my self-care sessions and they did not even know I was out of the house. I would ask my husband to look after them and upon my return, the kids were none the wiser that I had left.

This taught me a valuable lesson, how to regain my power, and how to massage and mold my power into what I needed it to be, which was to be able to take care of me. I needed to take care of me before I could have taken care of anyone else.

When my mind, my soul, my inner being and my spirit is in total harmony and in a happy place, my entire being is in a happy place. In and with self-treatment there is power, we just need to locate it, hone it, massage it and allow it to quantify itself into leaps and bounds. There is nothing better in this world than being a better you for the world.

*"Walk with pride knowing that you are who you are and
you are blessed each and every day."*
Cindy Bahadur-Ramkumar

Walking in the Power of Support

Just like there is power in numbers, so to there is power in support. Many would agree that the more people come together to support a cause, the more power there is in that group to sway the voice and opinion of the outcome.

Also, the more support that is available and accessible to you, the more you are able to thrive and succeed. The power of support could positively or adversely affect your outcome. Sometimes the support received is not always genuine and may have and include ulterior motives which can negatively impact the intended outcome. Having support is always a positive. Without support you can collapse, dwindle and fall over a period of time.

So what does having support mean? Having support means having people in your circle who have your back, having a group of friends who have a vested interest in obtaining a positive outcome for you. Having support also means there is someone at the other end of that line or phone call or text message willing share their personal time with you and willing to give you their undivided attention so that you are better able to express an opinion of your current situation to them.

Having support means you have a lifeline available to use at any point in your life, where you can make a phone call to that person who will be by your side in the shortest amount of time. Finally having support means having that one person who will check in on you constantly to make sure that you are OK and to make sure that you are doing what you say you will be doing, and that you are being held accountable for your actions, for your words, and for your deeds.

Throughout my life as far back as I can remember I have always had the support of my family, some friends and my husband. When life dealt me the most uncomfortable and difficult hand to deal with, I turned my back on my support. In 2012, I was dealt the worst blow that life could have given me. My life, even though it was riding high waves every day for all the years of my prior life, 2012 I was met with an extremely unfortunate circumstance and this became the low point in my life.

I knew I had the support of my friends and my family if I requested it, however I decided for my own sanity, in order to survive, I had to shut myself away from the world. This unfortunately meant that I was cutting my ties temporarily with my support group. It also unfortunately meant that I was going to ride the waves of this new disaster on my own without the help and support of anyone else. The last ten years of my life, even though there have been some good highs, it was plagued with many, many lows. My last ten years was filled with tears, sadness, pain, betrayal, death, poverty, and many unpredictable days.

"Use your POWER to help others, to restore happiness, to restore devotion, to restore goodness, to spread love, and greatness."

For the last ten years I lived only for my husband and my kids. They were the only beings that kept me going and the only ones who reminded me that I needed to be alive. During my time of turmoil, my expansive time of turmoil, I had shut myself away from the entire world and I lived only in my world. By shutting out the world directly and indirectly, I forced myself to live a life of solitude with my husband and kids. I did not have any financial or emotional support, I had no friends, I had no family, I had no one.

Even though my friends and my family were still around and available, I made it a priority to not answer any phone calls, to not be in touch with anyone, to avoid everyone, and to disappear from the world. I believe this was my method of coping and my way of shutting out the world to deal with my unbearable turmoil.

Shutting the world out was the only way I knew how to survive. This was also the only way I knew how to cope.

Disappearing from the world, meant I made a conscious decision to shut the world out and to cut out all the ties I had with everyone.

I did this because there were questions I did not have answers to, I did this because I was not able to confront anyone and finally I did this because it was the only way to save face and preserve my integrity at the same time.

Consciously losing all my support meant I lived in a world plagued with loneliness, pain, suffering, and injustices. I often wondered what life would have been like had I not barricaded myself in my own world, had I reached out to my support group of friends and family for assistance.

Many times, I wonder had I reached out to my immediate family and close friends when my life had taken a different road, would my current path have changed. One thing I can confirm and now know for sure, is having support generates many opinions and views on my life and my situation which I did not need and was not prepared mentally to manage.

I did not believe I was ready for everyone else's opinions and views on my life and my current situations. I believe that, had I taken the path of family and friends support, utilized the power within for the support given to me, my pain and my suffering might have been a little less, however I did not know if it would have ended. I also know with support I would have to live daily wondering what is next, who can I trust, and who has my back.

"Get hooked on your POWER, I guarantee you, once hooked there is no stopping your POWER acquisition drive."

I learnt earlier on in life that there is tremendous power and support out there. There is a wealth of people willing to assist you if you extend your hands out to them. I also learnt that people cannot assist you if there is no hand extended out to them.

I firmly believe there is power in support and I firmly believe that the majority of the members of your support team means no harm or have no ill will towards assisting you from whatever situation you encounter.

In my case, for the last ten years, I believe the only way I could have survived was building my walls really high and making sure that no one was able to climb over my walls to get to me. I am not sure if my support group and the power that they possessed to assist me would have helped me in any manner, based on my personality and the manner in which I keep my life very private, my support group would have failed in attempting to penetrate the high walls that I had built up and put around me.

I did however on many occasions use God as a means of

support and assistance. I normally would plead with God to send me someone who would just listen to me and not judge me and after I had that listening ear, have that person leave and we never cross paths again. Every time someone walked into my life who was there to listen to me and not judge me I found a way to build my walls even higher.

On many, many occasions an opportunity would present itself, where I was able to disclose my innermost feelings and be able to talk about what was going on in my life, as soon as the opportunity presented itself and I was asked what is going on or would you like to share with me what is on your mind, I often shut down and my answer was always no, I did not want to share my personal life with you.

It was as if I was asking for something and as soon as I received it I would give it away or no longer require it. I kept asking God to send me someone, send me a stranger that I can pour my heart out to, making sure we would never cross paths again. Fortunately, God had sent me strangers on numerous occasions. I had developed the courage to utilize their listening ear. Many, many times I would meet many new people who are strangers in my life. Unfortunately I was never able to disclose my life or speak about myself. These strangers ultimately became my friends and I could no longer share that part of me, or the part inside of me that was desperately trying to come out. Had I followed my heart and spoke about me to these strangers initially, I believe that I would have freed my mind and my thoughts from this world.

I know there is strength in numbers and there is strength in power. I have proven to myself over and over, with the right support all things are possible, and everything is possible. With the right group of friends, with the right ears to listen to you and with the right contributions from the supportive group anyone can conquer this world and fly as high as they need to fly.

There is power in support, just like there is strength in numbers. Having the right support makes a world of difference and will ultimately lead your life onto the right path. The right support will guide you, will care for you, will protect you, would look after your best interest, and will always have your back.

Having the right support is like having that little voice inside of your head which keeps telling you the right thing to do and keeps you on the correct path. That little voice in your head never ever takes you on the wrong path and that little voice in your head will always lead you on the right path to attain whatever you want to achieve in life. If that little voice in your head can get you to do an insurmountable, impossible task, having the right support group will lead you on the right path.

For anyone going through any type of tumultuous situations without any foreseeable end in sight, I urge you to please reach out to your support group, to please find those that are close to your heart who would understand you, not judge you and who would give you the best advice possible, so that you are better able to make an informed decision and you are in a better frame of mind mentally to move forward in life.

Do not be afraid to reach out to your support group, do not be afraid to advise that you need help, do not be afraid to ask for the advice, and most importantly do not be ashamed of your current situation.

Reach out and ask for help, reach out and ask for advice, reach out and do it with pride not embarrassment and finally reach out to that support group that is waiting for you to ring their doorbell so that they can open their hearts and share their minds with you.

There is power in support, you just have to know how to ask for assistance, when to ask for assistance and who to ask for assistance from.

"The world is your platform and the doors are open awaiting your presence, be brave, be bold and walk with your head held high through those doors."
Cindy Bahadur-Ramkumar

Walking in the Power of Self-Love

I decided that I wanted to end this book with the most important power that we possess. It is the power to love thy self.

It is my belief that having the innate power to love thy self is the most important power to have and to possess.

I always ask this question to my attendees, my students, and my participants, I asked them what does love mean and what does self-love mean? Is there a difference between love and self-love, and if there is a difference between love and self-love how does one get to the state of self-love?

As a child we are told to love thy neighbor, love thy self, and love all the people who are valuable and important to us in our life. We have all grown up in a world where we are able to love thy neighbor, because in so doing we are extending love to others to make sure that they feel good, that they are uplifted and that love is spread throughout the world.

I often tell my kids to share love, to extend love and to

make sure there is enough love to go around in the world. I tell my kids it does not cost anything to extend a hand to someone, to lend a listening ear to someone, to give a hug, and to make someone smile. After all, is this not why we were put in this world, to share love.

Even though we are all filled with multitudes and varying levels of love to share with everyone, we sometimes forget that we need to share love to ourselves. I am often guilty and always guilty of never extending self-love to myself. As with self-treatment, I do the same thing with self-love. I give of myself to everyone and when the time comes for me to give of myself to myself, I am normally tired, exhausted and have no more love to give to me.

"POWER is innate, find it, use it and shine with it."

Over the last ten years I have learnt that I am only as good to others as I am to myself. I have learnt that if I do not take care of me first there will be no more me. I have also learnt that throughout the roller coasters of life, if I have no love to give to myself then I become incapable of loving others fully, wholly and in the way that they should be loved.

My power of self-love came at a time when I needed it the most. The power of my self-love came when I had disappeared mentally and physically from this world, and I had no one to support me and no one to extend a hand out to me.

I learnt through trial and error that the only person who can love me is me. All my life I was taught, if you love someone unconditionally it is their responsibility to love you back unconditionally. This meant, if I give of myself in its entirety to someone, that someone must give of themselves in their entirety to me.

This false premise that I was taught earlier on in life, led me to many years of sadness and tears. It is only now I understand that I had given my power of self-love away to someone expecting them to return their power of self-love to me. It is only now I fully understand that the power of self-love belongs to me and me only, and there is no one out there who can and will love me as much as I can and will love myself.

It was a painful ten years of self-realization, self-love and self-witness to fully get to the stage where I am today, where I can truly profess with a hundred percent clarity that there is true power in self-love and there is true power in loving yourself wholly and unconditionally.

I am true testament to the word power and a true testament to everyone out there that power does exist and it emanates from within. Power allows me to shine my light brightly so the world can see me for who I truly am and was meant to be.

Had I not had this unfortunate situation imposed upon and onto me over a ten year span, I do not believe I would have reached the stage of true self-love, true self-acceptance, true self-confidence, and true clarity as it pertains to who I am and what my intended true purpose in this world was meant to be.

I was always told that there is a silver lining in every dark cloud, many days I longed and dreamt of that silver lining in my dark cloud. I could never find the silver lining and I could never reach the silver lining. I now know and fully understand that the only person that held me back from reaching that silver lining was me.

While I was busy giving my love to everyone else, while I was busy taking care of everyone else, and while I was busy being the best I can be for everyone else, I neglected me in this whole process.

I lost myself in a world of chaos and I did not know how to shine again, all I knew was how to survive. Now through this journey of writing this book, I am a hundred percent clearer in my purpose and have acquired a hundred percent clarity.

I am a willing participant in my journey off acquiring self-love and acquiring the true power that comes with self-love.

With this thing called life, a hand is dealt to you every day, the manner in which you play the hand that you are dealt with, will always determine the outcome of the game that you are playing.

It took me a long time to learn to play the right hand in life, however throughout this journey I have no regrets. I have learnt to become stronger, I have learnt more than anything else to be me and I have learnt to put myself first before I put anyone else first and in the process of putting myself first I have learnt to love myself again and to treat me as I expect to be treated and not wait for someone to treat me how I want to be treated.

The power of self-love is all encompassing, it is entirely whole and it truly belongs to you and you only.

No one can love you the way you can love yourself, and no one can put you before you. Only you can love you as you, and only you can give you what you desire and deserve in this life.

When you wait for others to give you what you deserve, what you expect, what you believe and what you need, you will always be disappointed because those who you depend on are not inside of your brain and they do not know your innermost thoughts, therefore they cannot fulfil your request without you discussing your request to them.

As a human race we are always disappointed and never satisfied. We are always disappointed because we place our love, happiness, contentment and life in the hands of others and expect them to love us the way we need to be loved. When others cannot fulfil our expectations of love, happiness and contentment, disappointment sets in, then argument ensues.

If we commit to understanding that we do not need others to make us happy and we only need ourselves to make us happy, life will be completely filled with love and void of disappointments. The only way we can learn to love ourselves truly is to surrender to ourselves and give ourselves and our inner beings a chance to live again.

The power of self-love comes from within and there is no greater satisfaction in this life than loving oneself unconditionally. There is no greater satisfaction in this life than taking care of oneself.

Seek the journey of true self-love and acquire the ability to understand that there is power in loving oneself, there is power and strength in becoming who you were truly meant to be.

Love yourself unconditionally in the same manner that you would love someone else, and treat yourself unconditionally with love in the same manner you would treat someone else, take care of yourself unconditionally in the same manner you would take care of someone else.

Finally walk upright and proud knowing that only you and you only possess the power within to love you as you and only you and you only possess the power that makes you who you are.

Yes there is no better feeling in this word and in this life than loving yourself conditionally and unconditionally.

There is power in self-love and there is self-love in power.

"Be good to you, love yourself."
Cindy Bahadur-Ramkumar

ABOUT THE AUTHOR

Cindy Bahadur-Ramkumar was born in Trinidad and resides in Canada. She is a Canadian Author **X7**

She is the Author of:

1. *101 Ways To Think Like A Business Person*

2. *The Struggle is Real*

3. *Changing U*

4. *Conversations*

5. *Pathway to Profit*

6. *Achieving Operational Excellence*

7. *Walking in MY TRUE POWER*

Cindy is the CEO and Founder of Management Systems &
Solutions.

She has built and taught businesses how to operate, sustain
and grow exponentially on zero (0) credit, streamlined and
consolidated businesses, coached businesses how to
maximize efficiencies and reduce cost all the while
maintaining a PROFIT.

Cindy is well known for creating structure in chaotic
business environments while implementing strategic
process improvements and business functionalities.

She imparts the know-how on how to aspire to have your
time equal more profit (time = more profit) and how to
achieve profitable status as a business owner.

Cindy is extremely knowledgeable, experienced and versed
in continuous improvements, organizational excellence,
operational excellence, metrics management, change
management, key performance indicators (KPI) and
maximizing efficiencies.

Cindy is a Linguist, Management System Auditor and
Consultant (HSSEQ - Health, Safety, Security,
Sustainability, Environment and Quality) by profession,

CINDY BAHADUR - RAMKUMAR

and is an Author, Reporter, Writer, Facilitator, Lecturer, Business Coach and Mentor.

To enhance your business potential and personal self, visit www.mssconsultants.com and email cindy@mssconsultants.com

The Good Stuff that you need to know about Cindy:

"You have a knack for wording and laying out processes very clearly." - L.D.

"You have changed my life, I worked with you for a year when my marriage and self-confidence was at its lowest, my marriage was in shambles and I was on the verge of a divorce. You coached me to be a better me and through being a better me, I was able to forgive, learnt to rekindle my marriage, purchase a new home for new beginnings and now I am expecting. You have become my sister rather than my friend." - R.C.

"Boss of Processes and Process Improvements." - A.M.

"I love reading you books, always enlightening." - I.B.

"Your books take me on unparalleled journeys of self-discovery, development and excellence, I am eagerly awaiting your next book" - A.R.

"Always fascinated by you, love hearing you speak, there is so much I can learn from you and your experiences." - G.C.

"Whenever you speak, I am like a sponge soaking up every last drop of your words, I could never ever get tired of listening to you, you have taught me how to chance my life for the better." - M.B.

"Believing you can change is half of the battle,
completing the change is the remainder of the battle."
Cindy Bahadur-Ramkumar

Your TRUE POWER
Notes

"Introduce yourself to your POWER and get hooked on your POWER."
Cindy Bahadur-Ramkumar

www.ingramcontent.com/pod-product-compliance
Lightning Source LLC
Chambersburg PA
CBHW071256220526
45468CB00001B/150